Increasing Faculty and Administrative Effectiveness

❖❖❖❖❖❖❖❖❖❖❖❖❖❖❖❖❖❖❖❖❖❖

Jack F. Heller

❖❖❖❖❖❖❖❖❖❖❖❖❖❖❖❖❖❖❖❖❖❖❖❖❖

Increasing Faculty and Administrative Effectiveness

❖❖❖❖❖❖❖❖❖❖❖❖❖❖❖❖❖❖❖❖❖❖❖❖

Jossey-Bass Publishers

San Francisco • Washington • London • 1982

INCREASING FACULTY AND ADMINISTRATIVE EFFECTIVENESS
by Jack F. Heller

Copyright © 1982 by: Jossey-Bass Inc., Publishers
433 California Street
San Francisco, California 94104
&
Jossey-Bass Limited
28 Banner Street
London EC1Y 8QE

Library of Congress Cataloging in Publication Data

Heller, Jack F.
    Increasing faculty and administrative effective-
ness.

    Bibliography: p. 121
    Includes index.
    1. Universities and colleges—United States—
Administration.   I. Title.
LB2341.H425   378'.1'0973   81-23663
ISBN 0-87589-520-4   AACR2

Manufactured in the United States of America

JACKET DESIGN BY WILLI BAUM

FIRST EDITION

Code 8210

A joint publication in
The Jossey-Bass Series
in Higher Education
and
in Social and Behavioral Science

Preface

Declining enrollments, financial pressures, changing institutional missions, and faculty whose skills and knowledge are out of date require colleges and universities to make major curricular, personnel, and organizational adjustments. Yet most attempts to change institutions of higher education ignore the most debilitating problems and the most sensitive issues. As a result, most attempted changes are ineffective and short-lived.

This book is intended to provide a unified approach to identifying and solving the fundamental problems that prevent colleges and universities from responding effectively to new demands. It demonstrates the underlying causes of institutional problems using case study examples of administrators and faculty members in their institutions. The book illustrates how to bridge the gap between insight about the causes of these problems and actions for solving them—actions that take into account the inertia and fear that typically plague efforts to change institutions of higher education. It shows that administrators and faculty members can learn to solve difficult institutional problems once and for all, instead of having to solve the same problems over and over again as they recur in new guises.

The book should help college and university presidents and deans evaluate the seriousness of the problems facing their institutions and the magnitude of effort required for solving them. It includes suggestions for assessing the capacity of their staffs to change and for determining whether programs offered by outside experts are likely to produce needed changes.

Faculty members should find the book helpful in understanding the causes of interdepartmental conflict and the reasons they often fail to communicate the perspectives of their disciplines to administrators. The book demonstrates how apparently isolated problems are related by common underlying causes, how faculty and administrative actions perpetuate problems, and what must be done to alter the persistent causes.

The case studies presented should help practitioners of institutional development understand why their best efforts to help colleges and universities are often met with indifference from faculty members and benign tolerance from administrators. Practitioners should also find interesting the broad analytic theory that is used to derive practical, direct actions for implementing change in complex organizations.

In Chapter One it is suggested that most efforts to address problems at colleges and universities represent repeated applications of ineffective principles—ineffective because they lead people to avoid the difficult, important issues that administrators and faculty members most want to address. The position is taken that the primary goal of any change effort should be to provide administrators and faculty members with the skills they need to identify and solve their own problems without continuous dependence on outside help. Principles for an approach to institutional problems consistent with that goal are presented.

Chapter Two is a case study of an ineffective effort by a small institution, "Liberal College," to solve the problem of reduced enrollment in particular departments with a high proportion of tenured faculty at a time of increased financial pressure. Everyone involved was committed to a balanced liberal arts curriculum and agreed on the need to make changes: nevertheless, efforts at rational adjustment produced resistance to change, faculty refusal to participate, departmental infighting, and the use of institutional power to impose change.

Chapter Three presents Argyris and Schön's *theory-of-action* as a tool for identifying and changing the characteristics of an institution that cause resistance to change and recurrence of problems. Theoretical concepts are introduced to account for administrators' and faculty members' tendencies to set goals that ignore others' needs; to manipulate others to create consensus; to discount resistance as maliciously motivated; and to withhold information and support. Several examples are used to illustrate the explanatory power of the concepts. These include the case of a professor who attempts unsuccessfully to improve her teaching and that of a university president who tries and fails to improve the managerial performance of a dean.

In Chapter Four the theory-of-action perspective is used to identify the causes of the continued conflict and ineffectiveness that characterized the change effort described in Chapter Two. The analysis specifies what led change advocates to use institutional power to apply for a grant without the support of potentially affected faculty members; why faculty members resisted the grant-sponsored program; why department heads released only their poorest teachers to the new program; and how the problems that occurred might have been anticipated. This analysis sets the stage for a detailed treatment of an alternative strategy for producing lasting, effective change.

Chapter Five follows a group of university administrators through a seminar in which they learn how to identify and solve basic institutional problems—by interrupting the ineffective problem-solving strategies they use automatically to achieve their goals and substituting strategies designed to unearth important, previously withheld information and to maximize individuals' internal commitment to policy decisions. They are able to do so through the use of heuristics. Heuristics are readily learned devices for breaking old action patterns and learning more effective ones. The seminar participants in Chapter Five gain skill in using these devices and eventually are able to design their own heuristics to solve institutional problems.

Chapter Six addresses the questions most frequently asked about the theory-of-action approach, makes clear the commitment and effort required to unlearn old patterns of behavior and learn new ones, discusses the kinds of institutional problems that are most readily solved by the approach, and points to the kinds of administrators and faculty leaders most likely and least likely to benefit from learning about the theory-of-action perspective. The chapter stresses that effective change must deal not only with specific problems but also with the basic problem-solving strategies of administrators and faculty members, because those strategies are common to a wide range of very different problems.

I owe several people a deep debt for giving me the intellectual perspective that made this book possible. Foremost of these is Chris Argyris, who gave me helpful advice at all stages of this project and made available the data collection on which Chapter Five is based. My thanks go also to Donald A. Schön for his skill as a teacher and for allowing me to use the case example in Chapter Two. The administrators and faculty of "Liberal College" deserve recognition for their openness and cooperation. My deep appreciation also goes to my colleagues for their sufferance of a long absence and to Mary Ann Russell for her patience and efficiency in preparing the manuscript. Perhaps most important is my acknowledgment to Sherri Heller, for her intellectual companionship and her shared joy in each new discovery.

I am grateful to the Andrew W. Mellon Foundation for their partial support of the leave of absence to Harvard University that made this book possible.

Lancaster, Pennsylvania
January 1982

Jack F. Heller

Contents

Contents

The Author

Jack F. Heller is associate professor of psychology at Franklin and Marshall College, Lancaster, Pennsylvania. He received his B.A. degree in psychology from the University of California, Los Angeles (1968) and his M.A. and Ph.D. degrees in social psychology from the University of Iowa (1970 and 1972, respectively). He recently spent two years as a postdoctoral fellow at Harvard University (1977–1979), where the research and most of the writing of this book were completed. Prior to his work with educational and industrial organizations, Heller conducted research on attitude change and crowding. His continued interests are organizational effectiveness and ecological approaches to social psychology.

To Michael Pallak
for showing me the joys of theoretical thinking

To Chris Argyris
for showing me a theory worth thinking about

Increasing Faculty and Administrative Effectiveness

❖-❖-❖-❖-❖-❖-❖-❖-❖-❖-❖-❖-❖-❖-❖-❖-❖-❖-❖

1

Current Approaches to Individual and Institutional Development

One of the primary purposes of institutions of higher education is to preserve, transmit, and add to our cumulative body of knowledge. The tremendous expansion of that knowledge within recent years has made the task ever more demanding. In the social sciences and the humanities as well as in the sciences, new areas of investigation and inquiry are regularly opened while established areas are consolidated or incorporated into new ones.

Until recently colleges and universities were able to keep up with the growth of knowledge by expanding. Federal funding, increasing enrollments, and private support made it possible to add new departments, to provide a steady influx of faculty with new orientations, and to steadily expand curricular offerings. While the basic body of knowledge continues to expand, however, federal funding and student populations have begun to shrink, and the

1

ability to keep abreast of changes has been sharply curtailed, threatening the capability of higher education to fulfill its role in society.

The Need for Inexpensive Revitalization

Given that continued expansion is impossible, most institutions of higher education have committed themselves to maintaining existing staff levels and academic offerings. As a result, new faculty can be hired only as existing faculty retire or leave. In institutions with a high proportion of tenured, middle-aged staff, this policy radically curtails the institution's ability to introduce new areas and perspectives through new faculty. Yet, it is essential to the academic health of such institutions that they be able to acquire faculty competent in new and emerging areas of knowledge.

Many institutions now face other painful facts: New programs can arise only from the ashes of old programs; new areas of knowledge can be represented in the curriculum only if existing faculty abandon or alter their current areas and take up new ones; better teaching can occur only if current faculty improve; and devoting more money to one discipline necessarily means less money for another.

Few within academic institutions fail to share a sense of dismay over their shrinking resources and increasing imperatives for change. Both faculty and administrators see that survival requires major changes. Administrative structures and procedures established during periods of economic plenty must be made more efficient and less costly. Poor teachers can no longer be ignored or assigned to nonteaching positions; today, most institutions can ill afford to sustain faculty who are not effectively contributing to the education of tuition-paying students. Finally, new areas of study that must be represented within the institution and the decrease in demand for others make it necessary to redistribute faculty positions among existing departments.

Despite a general awareness of the imperatives for change, attempts to innovate from within are inherently difficult. For example, if the history department needs more faculty while the sociology and anthropology departments must lose faculty and combine administratively, espoused interests in economy and collegiality may fall to disciplinary imperatives. Sociology and anthropology may resist because giving up faculty and combining administrations would compromise the integrity of their two disciplines, impoverish the training their students receive, diminish their autonomy, decrease their influence at faculty meetings, and reduce their claim to secretarial, teaching, and research funds. Simultaneously, the history department might argue that it cannot continue to teach courses with large enrollments, its majors are being short-changed faculty time, and its faculty cannot work on scholarly projects because of teaching demands. Almost any attempt to resolve this problem is likely to be seen as arbitrary, insensitive, and destructive by those adversely affected. The administration quickly comes to see the faculty in this situation as unreasonable, inflexible, and self-serving.

No one has sought these conflicts. Everyone has acted from the best motives: faculty to protect their disciplines and administrators to serve student interests and lower operating costs. Yet, the typical result is interdepartmental fighting over resources, animosity, and mistrust among faculty and between faculty and administrators. Although energy and time are devoted to defining problems, setting up task forces, and attending meetings of the faculty and administration, typically, some change is either forced on one segment of the institution by another or the process becomes so painful and disruptive that the effort to change is abandoned and the original problem left unsolved. Even if a compromise is accepted, it may fail to address the problem adequately and thus lead to another round of conflict. The most enduring effect of all the effort is that the faculty and the administration come to view productive change as impossible and institutional actions as self-destructive and counter to the academic interests of the faculty.

There appear to be two aspects of most efforts to change that generate conflict and negative reactions. The first is the particular problem that has made change necessary. The disproportion in enrollment between history and sociology-anthropology is a case in point. The second is the problems created by the actions taken to produce the needed change. Institutions have tended to focus on their immediate problems and have been rather bad at anticipating and dealing with unintended consequences of their efforts.

Although an institution can readily redistribute faculty positions, it can less readily cope with the adverse effects of a department's efforts to maintain its size and with the demoralization and resentment produced when it loses. Unawareness of such consequences is what has made change efforts appear to be universally disruptive and ineffective.

Relevance of Current Development Practices to Institutional Problems

The difficulties resulting from demands for innovation from within academic institutions have become the target of both research and action under the general rubric of institutional development, with most of the literature focusing on the restricted area of faculty development. The major proponents of development programs (Gaff, 1975, 1978; Bergquist and Phillips, 1975b, 1977) have sought to specify the nature of the problems and have advocated strategies for correcting them. Their first concern has been improving teaching. They recommend multifaceted programs for faculty renewal consisting of workshops, student evaluations of teaching, peer counseling, and the services of instructional improvement specialists. Their second concern has been called organizational development. Organizational development encompasses a variety of approaches, such as team building, conflict management, management by objectives, change contracting, and process consultation.

Practitioners of organizational development have considerable insight into the problems facing academia, and many colleges and universities have tried at least some of their methods. But despite the diversity of approaches and their increasing use, there is little evidence of significant change and some evidence that basic problems remain untouched.

For example, systematic efforts to improve teaching are frequent, but surveys (Centra, 1976, 1977) suggest that they have not succeeded in many cases because the faculty who most need to improve do not use the programs. When these poor teachers are tenured, there are few institutional ways to motivate them to change. They are perceived by their peers and the administration as uninfluenceable and are subsequently left to teach a few small seminars.

The failure of this small group either to attract students or contribute to the reputation of the institution through their research is a basic institutional problem that current teaching improvement efforts have not addressed. The cost of nonproductive faculty members is tremendous in terms of money and reputation; one such person can cost an institution up to a million dollars in a ten-year period, and many such persons have twenty to thirty years until retirement. The burden is probably unacceptable if even two to three percent of the faculty represent this extreme problem.

Similar lack of success follows from programs intended to address institution-level problems. It is difficult to see how the approach articulated by Bergquist and Phillips (1975b, 1977), Bergquist and Shoemaker (1976), and others can do anything about the most difficult problems facing colleges and universities. It seems unlikely that their abstract discussions of leadership characteristics, exercises for active listening, paper-and-pencil team games, or value clarification activities can help institutions solve their most serious problems. These approaches seem irrelevant to problems such as financial and enrollment pressures, conflict caused by increased faculty militancy, eroded institutional purpose, or the need to improve or create academic programs. In fact, Centra's surveys indicate that institution-level change efforts are very infrequent, and that those that have been used have failed to address the most debilitating problems. These failures suggest a need for some alternative methods. The explication of a model for producing change in colleges and universities is the focus of this book.

Two Perspectives on Development Activities

It is possible to analyze current development practices from the viewpoint of practitioners, faculty, or administrators. Practitioners, from their perspective, seek the most effective ways to produce change. They use certain principles and strategies to guide their actions and to design their programs. Administrators and faculty, however, may view those programs in ways other than the practitioners had intended. This section treats some of the salient features of current development efforts and illustrates how practitioners and institution members might interpret those features.

Comparing different interpretations of the same actions can reveal why some programs fail while development staff remain unaware of the reasons for the failure.

The field of faculty development encompasses a wide range of strategies that development teams use to achieve their goals, but several common assumptions underlie most current development efforts. For example, current approaches stress the need for initiators of new programs to make as tangible as possible the institution's commitment to development. It is widely suggested that any center or program should have its core activities and staff financed as a regular part of the institutional budget, since development financed by "soft" money or discretionary funds is subject to quick cancellation. Other common assumptions include the advisability of beginning with low-risk projects (for example, voluntary teaching improvement efforts) while holding off on high-risk ones (for example, curricular planning at the departmental level) to most quickly make new programs a part of the institutional environment. Offering whatever peripheral services faculty might request, such as making slides or preparing demonstration materials (Gaff, 1975, 1978), should favorably dispose faculty toward a development program. Evaluating faculty only on self-selected aspects of their teaching will reduce anxiety about evaluation. The general principle is to offer services that do not pressure faculty. All these strategies are based on a gradual approach to development; change efforts begin small, gradually build trust, and reduce defensiveness through successful treatment of lesser issues. It is assumed that development personnel can increase trust and develop a working relationship so that faculty will eventually address their more serious problems.

Development Personnel's View. The strategies and principles mentioned above represent what might be called a "service model" for institutional development. This is the model that guides most professional development consultants. They see colleges and universities as needing a range of services to help them improve both teaching and institutional functioning in general. They assume that the need for such services exists now and for the foreseeable future, that it is important to provide only the level of service requested by the institution, that institutions (and their members) will either come to see their need for additional services or come to trust the consultants and ask for higher level services.

What are the likely consequences of this model? Let's look at the principle "Don't pressure the faculty." Development personnel operating on this principle would not attempt to force or persuade a faculty member to take a particular course of action. They would not say, "There are much better ways to teach than the way you do now," because of the implied threat to the faculty member's self-esteem and sense of competence. Instead, they might publicly agree with the faculty member's self-evaluation of his teaching even if serious teaching problems were evident and even if agreeing communicated an unintended message at odds with the goals of the development effort.

The existence and nature of messages implicit in actions are not adequately treated in the service model. When a development specialist publicly agrees with a faculty member's self-assessment, he or she may have achieved the goal of not threatening a faculty member. Unfortunately, that faculty member may reasonably have made the following inference: "I thought all along that I could identify and deal with my own minor teaching problems. My consultation with this expert confirms that belief." As a consequence, he or she may perceive no need either for using additional development services or for attempting to find more serious problems. The effort to avoid a threat may also have reaffirmed the faculty member's belief that his or her teaching needs no improvement. The more the faculty member needs to change, the more serious are the consequences of such an inference.

Development personnel subscribing to the principles of the service model conceive of themselves as service providers, but tend to be unaware of potential contradictions inherent in their actions and blind to the importance of their unintended messages.

Faculty and Administration Views. Faculty and administrators, however, are often aware of these contradictions because they continually use the development staff's actions to learn about the staff's goals and strategies for achieving them. Faculty and administrators evaluate any program in terms of its ability to increase their institution's effectiveness. Juxtaposing what institution members seek to learn with the service model helps reveal some of the unintended consequences of current development methods. Consider that to be effective (i.e., to achieve some desired objective), one must learn to detect and correct errors in goal-directed action. By the time a development program has been invited to a campus, it is likely that members of the institution have already learned that (1) they have problems with teaching or institutional functioning and (2) they do not have the skills to identify and change the causes of the problems themselves. Development specialists would be invited to campus specifically to address those problems. From the development team faculty expect (1) to learn more about the sources of inefficiency or error than they have been able to learn on their own, and (2) to learn approaches to or solutions for problems that are better than the ones they were able to produce for themselves. Naturally they also want to know if the development consultants have the skills to produce solutions and how they intend to go about correcting the problems that have been too difficult for the institution to handle on its own.

Faculty and administrators will observe what actions consultants take and sift out for themselves the underlying meanings. If they correctly infer from the effort to make funding a regular budget item that the team intends to make development activities a permanent part of the institution, then they will have learned at least two things from the perspective of their own needs. Given that competition among departments for funds is endemic to higher education, faculty will have learned that the development effort is going to become a permanent part of that competition. However justified the rationale for permanent status, such a development program would become part of one of the major problems confronting the institution, since departments would now face added competition from the development effort. The result is an inner contradiction. Development personnel try to act on the principle "do not pressure or threaten faculty," yet the program itself is perceived as a very real economic threat.

Something else may well have been learned. The institution has problems which it wishes to eliminate. If the problems no longer exist, then there is no need for the continued existence of the development program. Yet by its actions, the development program has indicated that it should be a permanent feature of the institution. One implication of a permanent development effort is that the institution's problems will always exist. If the institution's problems are unsolvable, it is certainly reasonable to ask why the team should be hired in the first place. If the team can solve problems, the wish to become a permanent fixture in the institution might lead to the inference that one of its objectives is to secure permanent employment; development staff are then likely to be suspected of making unnecessary work to justify their positions. Finally, if they can solve problems, it is understandable that they would seek permanent employment only if additional problems would frequently arise and would require their expertise. If this were true, then the members of the institution will have learned that they are never going to be able to solve their own problems and will always be dependent on their resident experts for solutions.

The difficulty of producing effective change is compounded when development personnel are unaware of the contradictions that their actions produce in the eyes of institution members. If the team does not discuss these contradictions, it can only be assumed that the team is aware of them and does not want to discuss them. A sincere development effort may meet resistance and generate hostility not for what the development team does or says, but for issues it has created but failed to address. The conclusion that members of an institution may well reach is that the development team is playing a game in which it is more concerned with its own survival than with improving the institution's ability to solve problems.

Unintended Consequences of the Service Model

Single-Loop Learning. There are several important implications of the service model and its effects: (1) It produces effects of which those using the model are unaware. (2) Practitioners may reinforce existing institutional problems. (3) When the problem does surface in the form of inability to deal with existing issues or exacerbation of current problems, the new problem is typically approached by applying the same model that created the situation. The inability to examine the causal role of one's own model and the continual application of a model that does not address or, in fact, contributes to the problem is characteristic of *single-loop problem solving* or *single-loop learning* (Argyris and Schön, 1974).

Single-loop learning is analogous to the functioning of a room thermostat. When the temperature reaches a certain level, the thermostat detects this state and acts to change it. It can continually and repeatedly apply this principle when an "error" (temperature change) has occurred and correct it. However, a thermostat cannot learn about and act to correct anything outside the range of its programming. For example, the thermostat would be useless in addressing the "error" in effective heating that would be created if residents went on vacation or if gas or oil were no longer being delivered to the furnace. The device cannot assess and address the limiting effects of its internal principles. The principles of the service model discussed earlier (e.g., don't threaten the faculty; get regular budget support) function in much the same way. Within the range of action to which they are relevant, they function well and effectively. But when practitioners adhere to the principles cited, they are unable to detect and correct certain consequences of their own and institutional members' behavior. Such single-loop processes are the basis of ineffective problem solving by faculty, administrators, and development teams.

To detect errors in one's model for action requires that one engage in *double-loop learning* or problem solving (Argyris and Schön, 1974). Double-loop learning involves the ability to inquire into and specify the principles that guide one's behavior and to determine their consequences. If there are unintended consequences, then one must have the skills to construct new principles. It is a central notion of the theory-of-action that most current problem-solving behavior is single loop in nature. That is, actions are guided by tacit principles and have consequences of which one is unaware. The tacitness and unawareness continually reinforce one's inability to act outside of one's current theory-of-action. To be able to engage in double-loop problem solving, one must be able to make explicit, examine, and change one's theory-of-action.

An Action Gap. Another important consequence of current approaches to change in higher education stems from particular techniques. Specifically, because of any of a number of "good" reasons, development activities seldom focus on the institution's at-home environment. Rather, they deal with issues and problems indirectly. If two departments are in conflict, for example, the development team might decide that the problem is a failure to cooperate and then teach about cooperation by discussing hypothetical situations and by using related simulations. The relevant issues may be treated through such simulations as Prisoner's Dilemma Games, which can provide insight into the negative consequences of competition and give some appreciation of how effectiveness can be increased through cooperation. Even though such insights can be an important source of satisfaction for participants, trouble lies in translating the lessons learned in such simulations to the participant's own environment. One may have learned to choose the cooperative response (of two possible responses) in the Prisoner's Dilemma Game, but an infinite number of possible responses exist in one's institution, and it is not clear which one is most cooperative. Furthermore, others may not share one's evaluation of the payoffs or may have a completely different view of the problem. For example, if others see the problem as your ignorance of the issues rather than a lack of cooperation, not only are your efforts at cooperative behavior ineffective, but your insights are irrelevant.

Nothing in the simulations or games used by development teams teaches participants either how to bridge this gap from insight to action or how to deal with the gap between their own and others' perceptions of the problem. Bridging this gap requires techniques for linking insight to action. Current development efforts tend to be relatively good at producing insights into the abstract nature of the problems, but they lack a methodology for bridging the gap between those insights and the actions that would produce effective change, and are, therefore, largely incapable of teaching how to produce effective action.

Principles for an Alternative Model

The theory-of-action perspective on development that will be fully discussed in Chapter Three makes a number of assumptions. First, change is successful when an institution increases its own effectiveness at identifying and correcting problems. Second, effective change requires that institutions analyze their patterns of decision making, control, and interaction, since many problems are entwined in taken-for-granted patterns of action. Third, since individuals within the institution are both the source of errors and conflict and the ultimate resource for correcting them, it is impossible to alter error-producing action patterns or to solve institutional problems unless patterns of individual action and reaction are examined in relation to the problems. Fourth, the roots of truly difficult problems are deeply embedded in everyday institutional functioning. Human beings are good at perpetuating organizational routines but relatively poor at reflecting on the unintended consequences. Increasing effectiveness requires specifying the aspects of routine action that produce unintended, unwanted consequences and altering the individual processes underlying the actions.

The unintended consequences and ineffectiveness of the service model of development are unavoidable, given the principles upon which it is based. The theory-of-action approach is based on three principles intended to eliminate many of the undesirable consequences of current development efforts and provide an alternative framework for approaching the problems of colleges and universities.

According to this approach effective faculty development occurs to the extent that an institution develops the skills to identify and solve its own problems and reduces its reliance on the skills of professional development personnel. Thus the first principle of this alternative approach is: *Effective development occurs as institutions learn to identify and solve their problems.* Whether it is increasing teaching effectiveness, dealing with departmental conflicts, or avoiding the paralytic effects of institutional allocation fights, an effective institutional development program teaches individuals to become their own problem solvers. Effective programs for change are designed not just to solve specific problems, but to teach institutional members how to discover the roots of their own problems, plan solutions, and enact those solutions in such a way that the problems remain solved. To acquire such skills requires time, effort, and a high commitment to learning. Faculty and administrators must be willing to analyze their own actions, discover what creates ineffective actions, and then design more effective patterns of interaction. Initially participants may be highly dependent on the development staff, but as learning increases, their need for assistance will decrease.

In contrast to the gradualism of current development models, the theory-of-action approach advocates that development personnel make their goals and assumptions explicit from the beginning, specify the problems that the model focuses on, show how those problems might be reflected in the institution, and demonstrate the actions that will change the conditions producing the problems. Thus the second principle is this: *Development personnel must be able (1) to create an environment in which institutions can test for themselves the validity of the approach and the analysis and solutions it produces and (2) to demonstrate how the client can learn to deal effectively with the problem.* Since institutions undertake change programs to identify and solve their problems, everything taught by a development team should be relevant to that basic need. That means a two-fold responsibility for development personnel. First, they must be able to demonstrate that their approach is capable of discovering more about the nature of institutional problems than it is possible for members of the institution to discover on their own. Second, they must be able to help institutional members test how all the exercises, applied theory, and data collection advocated are relevant to increased effectiveness in dealing with the problems discovered.

Finally, the third principle for an alternative approach: *A change effort must include a plan for specifying the underlying causes of institutional problems and techniques that translate understanding into effective action.* It is necessary to have some means of filling the gap between insight and action. This gap filling is not a trivial problem. It is typical in higher education to hear faculty and administrators describe their problems with some insight. They see that they are in conflict and should cooperate with one another, that departmentalism is divisive and should be assuaged, that conflicting demands on their time reduce effectiveness, and that they should become better organized. These insights and the realization of associated negative consequences are sometimes painful, but usually not terribly difficult, especially in organizations composed of people with highly developed conceptual and analytical ability. The problem is not in knowing, but in doing. If insight were a sufficient condition for increasing effectiveness, there would be little need for any development or change programs. An adequate development model must include both components of effective action to be useful to colleges and universities.

2

❖-❖-❖-❖-❖-❖-❖-❖-❖

Ineffective
Institutional
Problem Solving:
A Case Study

❖-❖-❖-❖-❖-❖-❖-❖-❖-❖-❖-❖-❖-❖-❖-❖-❖-❖-❖

This chapter describes one institution's efforts to produce major changes in its faculty and curriculum. It focuses as much as possible on directly observable actions and their consequences for the individuals involved. The material for this case derives from interviews with faculty and administrators; memorandums and other documents written by those involved; a description of events, compiled from observation and participants' interviews; and tape recordings of several meetings. Although information collected and presented in this manner is always subject to selection and unintended distortion, I have tried to provide sufficient quotations and excerpts from documents to minimize the distortion. The assumption behind my reporting of this case is that because problems result from specific actions one must know what the actions were to understand the cause of a problem and how to correct it.

This case is divided into ten episodes. Each episode represents, roughly, one iteration of a single-loop strategy for change. While a theoretical analysis of the single-loop qualities of the case follows in Chapter Four, two points are worth making here. First, although the specific actions in each episode are very different, the causes of the actions are very similar across the ten episodes. Second, although errors made in the first episodes are relatively straightforward and their consequences easily identifiable, in subsequent episodes the uncorrected errors begin to be compounded, their consequences become more serious, and create problems that begin to ripple through the institution. Ultimately, the original problem and its basic causes are obscured by the urgency of dealing with the newest problem.

Background: The Problems of the Foreign-Language Departments

"Liberal College" is a high-quality, four-year liberal arts institution. Approximately 60 percent of its graduates go on for advanced degrees in academic disciplines, law, medicine, or business.

The administration and faculty of Liberal College have publicly taken the position that curricular and financial challenges should be met with reasoned boldness, not trepidation. In an uncertain financial environment, the college has sought to foster interdisciplinary programs, such as American Area Studies, History and Philosophy of Science, and a Cultures of Europe Program. It has met a countercurrent of resistance to any change from a minority of the faculty. As one administrator indicated, some faculty, especially in the foreign languages, are inclined to withdraw from anything new. Overall, however, Liberal College is characterized by an administration willing to initiate and support change and by a faculty which has avowed that it is ready to change.

In the late 1960s and early 1970s, several factors internal and external to the college began to affect the faculty and the institution. Prior to the nationwide trend, the faculty voted to remove the foreign language graduation requirement. Naturally the immediate effects of this change were felt by foreign language departments, whose staffing levels and teaching loads had been structured in line with the expectation that a high percentage of the student body would at some time enroll in their courses. When the requirement was removed, enrollments dropped dramatically, presenting these departments with three overriding concerns: how to keep individual faculty members within the department active and engaged in the rewarding professional life they had trained for and enjoyed up to that point; how to justify continuing their current level of staffing; and how to maintain their disciplinary identity and *esprit de corps.*

The college also took steps to balance its budget, trying to affect the functioning of the institution as little as possible. One such action was to reduce the total number of faculty. Areas serving relatively fewer students lost proportionally more faculty, and so language departments were hit most heavily; nontenured faculty were not retained and retiring senior faculty were not replaced. Worry over additional cuts in staffing led faculty into a numbers race. Program integrity for tenured faculty and personal security for nontenured faculty seemed to lie in teaching more students (by various indices) than other departments. Throughout the institution and especially in the foreign language departments, competition for enrollment increased.

Despite individuals' preferences and the institution's stance, the consequence was a temporary swing in the pendulum of academic philosophy toward a market notion of academic functioning. Aspects of this competitive idea were an increase in the number and variety of courses offered, an apparent increase in course redundancy, and allegations that faculty inflated grades so as to attract students. Again, while universal, these phenomena were most apparent where pressures were greatest—in the modern foreign languages. To make matters worse, fear that the financial situation might worsen raised the prospect that staff might be reduced to the point that departments could not maintain their curricular integrity. In fact, with the drastic drop in both staff and enrollments, language faculty were already hard pressed to maintain their disciplinary programs while attracting students with non-foreign language course offerings.

The desire to maintain the language staff presented the administration with a conflict between solvency and a liberal education. Financial logic indicated that further reductions should fall most heavily on the foreign language departments because they had the fewest students. Educational logic argued that further reductions in the languages' staff would threaten the existence of foreign language programs and endanger the college's viability as a liberal arts institution.

The foreign language faculty faced an equally difficult dilemma. If they responded only to numbers, they would have to offer whatever courses would attract students. Since such courses were not likely to be foreign language and literature, a pragmatic response would require radical alterations of their programs and would clearly violate their values and beliefs about the conduct of their discipline. Failure to increase enrollments, however, might just as effectively eliminate their ability to offer an acceptable curriculum.

Unable to pursue either course wholeheartedly, the foreign language faculty responded in a way that allowed them to maintain their own values: They stretched themselves thin to cover the heart of the foreign language curriculum and at the same time add elective nonlanguage courses in history, culture, art, and literature in translation. On average, each language department faculty member at Liberal College took on two additional course preparations after the language requirement was dropped. Preparation time and work increased, the direction of careers diffused, morale decreased, and competition for enrollment increased.

Throughout this entire adjustment the foreign language faculty adhered to its existing values about and goal for foreign language study. A composite statement of this goal, inferred from the interviews with language faculty, is as follows: The study of a foreign language is intended to aid in understanding and appreciating the culture, values, and history of another country through its language, literature, and cultural documents and to use that world view as a mirror to enlighten aspects of one's own heritage and culture.

According to the theory-of-action perspective introduced in Chapter One, faculty should consistently work toward achieving this goal and resist efforts to minimize their effectiveness. Within this imperative, curricula might vary somewhat, but major changes inconsistent with this basic value would be regarded as clearly unacceptable.

Episode 1: The First Attempt to Resolve the Dilemma

The administration sought to avoid choosing between financial expediency and the needs of the foreign languages' academic program by seeking outside funds to support the language departments. As one administrator put it, a way was sought to "get money so that we would not have to make the cuts in faculty as drastic as we would otherwise have had to do. This would allow us to excuse the languages from the rigors of the numbers game. We hoped this would allow the languages to design a program with academic integrity and one useful to them in a pragmatic way."

Juxtaposing this statement with the following excerpt from the grant proposal that was eventually written makes it clear that the institution sought a nonlanguage program for its foreign language faculty: "The classics department, imperiled no less than the foreign languages by the abandonment of a requirement, overcame its malaise by reinterpreting its function. Not merely the custodian of ancient languages and literatures, classics now offers as well courses in ancient myth, archeology, historiography, and political thought."

A large granting agency offered a program grant which roughly fit the college's needs, and administrators saw it as a possible source of money. While the effort to get this grant involved a number of humanities departments at Liberal College, this case will focus on the modern foreign languages because they were clearly in the greatest distress and because their need was the impetus for initiating the grant-seeking process. Also, the foreign languages' opposition to the program is prototypical of resistance to change in higher education. The administration hoped that the language faculty would welcome the prospect of external support to provide temporary relief from pressures caused by the loss of students. A primary condition of the grant was that any funded program have no language requirement. The initial possibility of grant money seemed to interest language departments greatly, and several faculty members met and discussed how a program for the study of Europe might be structured. They then sketched a few program proposals, and while these varied in detail all centered around the study of language.

Episode 2: Reaction to the Languages' Initial Efforts

These sketchy proposals were reviewed by the administrator overseeing the grant effort. He reiterated that the granting agency explicitly forbade any but the most minimal language requirement and that any program which did have a strong language component would be unlikely to bolster foreign language enrollments or otherwise help the departments. He suggested that the faculty draft other proposals consistent with that guideline.

On the whole, the language faculty saw such a restriction as unacceptable. As one senior faculty member put it: "I was under the impression that it [the grant] was an effort to help the language departments. I wanted the program to include language study. When I found the agency was not interested in funding language study, my enthusiasm for the program dropped."

With a few notable exceptions, the language faculty lost interest in any grant application. No language department or any subgroup of the language faculty tried to produce a different proposal. The administration's idea of a Cultures of Europe Program that did not center around language study was not acceptable in light of the departments' existing values. As a result, they did not respond to administrative efforts to reinterest them in outside money. One administrator said she became "disappointed that the foreign languages didn't take the initiative, because it seemed that the grant was a device to let the languages come on."

The withdrawal of the language faculty from the fund-seeking effort was a critical incident. The reasons for and the dynamics of this event need to be understood for two reasons. First, the underlying pattern of this episode is repeated throughout the Cultures of Europe effort, which lasted three years. Understanding the pattern may illuminate many of the reasons for subsequent events. Second, the language faculty's withdrawal from and subsequent hostility to a Cultures of Europe grant reflects an important paradox: These departments desperately needed support in order to protect their discipline and their jobs, yet they apparently made no effort to win a grant that would provide that protection.

It seems reasonable to assume that the language departments' response made sense to them, since human beings do not intentionally act in ways that produce incongruity and paradox. From their perspective, help for the languages would involve maintaining or increasing their ability to teach foreign languages and literature. The restriction on language study therefore violated their basic values and did nothing to provide the help they felt they needed. In their view, the grant was useless to them.

Episode 3: The Drafting Committee

Because he wished to find support to preserve and encourage humanistic study, the dean of the college appointed a Drafting Committee and charged them with writing a grant proposal after the language faculty lost interest. Since the languages had made clear that they had no interest in a program without a core of language study, the dean did not appoint any of their faculty to the committee. All faculty who were appointed to the Drafting Committee believed that outside support was imperative for the humanities in general and the languages in particular. At this stage, the committee viewed the language faculty as feeling vulnerable and threatened, but thought they would eventually see the need for outside aid and would cooperate with any academically sound program which brought that aid. With those beliefs to support them, the committee tried to draft a sound proposal consistent with the granting agency's guidelines. The languages responded to the committee with largely negative attitudes:

- There was a minimum of input from the [language] departments. The committee which did the proposal was unrepresentative. The individual departments were not consulted and/or their advice was not taken.
- People on the committee weren't departmental representatives.
- The proposal was made by interested parties, but I don't think departments had much of a role in the proposal. In fact, many faculty and departments were opposed to the idea.

These comments reflect the consequences of the dean's effort to resolve his dilemma. Nevertheless, the dean felt little choice but to continue the grant proposal effort.

Although the language departments did not wish to work with the committee, they reacted negatively to their exclusion from it. They had acted in a way which ensured that a Drafting Committee would be appointed without their participation and then took the administration to task for the composition of that committee. Since they had withdrawn interest and contact on the issue, their reactions were seldom heard by committee members.

Episode 4: The Language Departments React

The committee was sufficiently concerned about the level of support for a grant effort that it attempted to evaluate campuswide interest and solicited brief proposals from any faculty who wished to participate. The committee had initially taken the position that it would integrate as many proposals as possible into one program. When twenty-two proposals were received from fifteen different departments, the committee judged that sufficient interest existed to propose and eventually staff a program should the grant be awarded.

Despite this apparent support for its aims, the committee was worried about possible resistance throughout the college and especially within the humanities. While there was some sentiment among committee members that resistance reflected the predisposition of some language faculty to oppose any change, memos written by the Drafting Committee suggest that it was concerned about generating support to overcome resistance from various segments of the college: "Part of the reason the college was advised to withdraw its first proposal [for a smaller grant two years previously from the same agency] was because of a deficiency in faculty, student, and administration support and/or participation. . . . Given the unfortunate results and faculty suspicions related to the serious lack of collegewide consultation on the last proposal, the Drafting Committee must do a lot of time-consuming grass roots consultation with individual departments. . . . It will take considerable face-to-face persuasion to try to overcome the growing faculty isolationism caused, in part, by roster fear [staff cuts] and also by what is perceived as the college's increased emphasis on professionalism [publications, national reputation, etc.]." Committee members subsequently met with chairpersons of all college departments, including science and social science departments, to explain the purpose of the grant, allay fears, and undertake necessary persuasion.

One member of the committee who had a special understanding of and sympathy for the language departments met with them in an effort to "bring them around," as he put it, and he reported to the committee that he believed they would support the current grant effort. As we shall see, this was an overoptimistic evaluation. In deciding to continue with a proposal, the committee invited nine faculty members to join a number of subcommittees to work the numerous proposals into a coherent package. While these faculty members worked closely with the Drafting Committee, the committee itself had little further contact with academic departments.

The Drafting Committee maintained contact with the subcommittees by putting a Drafting Committee member on each subcommittee. While this was an efficient method of organization, it meant actual work on the grant proposal was now done by a small segment of faculty. That group concentrated on developing the proposal and minimized consultation with departments and other faculty. This lack of communication was reinforced by faculty members' belief that the committee would incorporate their brief proposals, and hence their interests, into the grant and, again, by the withdrawal of the foreign language departments. As a result, little feedback from the faculty was used in developing the details of the proposed program, and faculty outside the drafting groups knew little about the evolving proposal. The committee structure minimized broader input into the proposal and cut the drafters off from further information about faculty preferences and reactions. The first draft of the proposal was largely based on ideas from a small number of the faculty. The Drafting Committee circulated the draft to departments and then met with them to get their reactions.

The meeting with the language departments attracted about one third of their faculty. Most members who had earlier expressed disapproval did not attend. While the granting agency forbade using the grant as a vehicle to reintroduce a language requirement, it did permit some language study as part of a larger program. Thus, part of the discussion with the language departments focused on the language requirement for majors as written into the draft of the

Cultures of Europe Program. Language faculty believed that all students in the proposed new major should have either language skills equivalent to six semesters of language study or some competence with two foreign languages. Since these positions did not match the grant guidelines, the Drafting Committee would not write them in, but did not tell that to the language faculty. Instead, they agreed to refine the proposal to include the concerns about language competence.

While it is not possible to be certain in retrospect, the memo below makes it seem likely that the language faculty left this meeting with the belief that their position on language study would be adopted in the final version of the proposal. This memo resulted from a meeting of the modern foreign language council held to formalize their view of the language requirement. It read, in part: "The consensus of the foreign language council centered around these points: (1) Students must be given the tools to approach foreign cultures in their most complex, significant, and intimate expression: their language. (2) The goals of language study in the Cultures of Europe Program are: (a) high competence in written comprehension. . . ; (b) excellent oral comprehension, and fluency in language. . . . (3) The competence level in foreign language can be defined as comparable to but not identical with a sixth semester in the foreign languages. . . . The competence test will be designed by the foreign language council." The position of the language council is clear and it reiterates the position that was unacceptable to the Drafting Committee.

Episode 5: Reactions to the Drafting Committee's Proposed Program and the Submitted Proposal

The committee received the language council's memo, but did not respond to it because of meetings already scheduled with all other departments in the college and because of the quickening pace of events. Meetings of the Drafting Committee with other departments were evoking more negative reactions. The committee was taken to task for not consulting more with them; the approach to Cultures of Europe was described as old-fashioned and lacking in coherent methodology (which could be supplied by incorporating the current approaches of relevant faculty); content areas of interest to some faculty were not represented; and there was too much emphasis on creating new courses. As in its meeting with the language departments, the committee noted faculty concerns and assured everyone that the committee would try to work with departments in revising the proposal.

These meetings made it apparent that, despite the committee's efforts to provide a structure to the proposal-writing process allowing maximum participation by faculty, significant segments of the college felt that their opinions had been neither sought nor used. Pragmatically this meant that some faculty members objected to the proposal to the extent that their interests were not represented in it. This made an impossible burden for the Drafting Committee. To respond to everyone's interests would produce a program that incorporated everyone's current skills and area of expertise. The result would be a curriculum which differed little, if any, from that already in place; but one purpose of the grant was to produce a program that did differ from the present curriculum, especially with regard to foreign languages. A new program would require faculty to change what they were doing, whereas the faculty wanted to do what they had always done (e.g., teach language or use current analytic methodology) within a new program. This is one aspect of a central theme recurrent throughout the effort to design and enact the Cultures of Europe Program: Individuals approach change by trying to determine how to make a new situation consistent with their old approach rather than by examining and changing their approach.

Shortly after all the meetings had been held, the Drafting Committee and a representative of the college administration met with the grant officer to review the proposal. The meeting was highly distressing. The grant officer was very critical of the proposal and maintained that it lacked a cohesive philosophy, that its goals and internal structure were unclear, and that it was a ho-hum idea. He also maintained that support of the relevant departments was not evident from the material presented, that there was little evidence of "deep curricular change" coming from the program, and that an in-depth examination of the existing curriculum had not been made. As a result of this meeting, the proposal had to be drastically changed, and the approaching submission deadline made further consultation with faculty impossible. The committee quickly rewrote the application and submitted it.

The final proposal presented an analysis of the college prior to the grant effort to highlight the needs and goals of the program and the current state of the college:

> Statistical analysis by department and division demonstrates a shift in the last five years away from the languages and some of the humanities departments. The current proposal is designed to produce a reverse of this shift, to allow retention and strengthening of the faculty in the humanities and humanistically oriented social studies.
>
> The economic viability of these [language] departments—that is to say, their ability to lay claim on financial resources—has been severely weakened. The plight of the humanities may therefore be seen as a failure to channel students into those courses and areas once considered so essential to their education that they were legislated into them.
>
> With the implementation of this proposal—the college could consolidate its gains, restore curricular balance, revitalize its faculty, and provide an excellent and attractive humanities program to the entire student body.

Based on this analysis the proposal presented a program with the following objectives and strategies for meeting them: "(1) *Unity.* The program is grounded in an integrated approach to humanistic study, one that is not merely internally coherent, but that sustains connections with other parts of the curriculum. . . . (2) *Elimination of redundancy in course content.* The sources of such redundancy are the absence of divisional curricular planning and the competitiveness to recruit students for a department. The proposed program makes more rational use of faculty resources. (3) *Stimulus to innovation and development.* The program provides incentives for continuing experimentation in courses and methodology consistent with the program's overall objectives. (4) *Relief to areas of greatest distress.* Without reimposition of course requirements, the program will help restore dignity and purpose to foreign language study."

Under the heading of institutional support, the proposal indicated that the college, in order to ensure the program's success, must make strategic changes in admissions, counseling, placement, faculty recruitment, and departmental organization. The last of these is most relevant to the change effort: *"Departmental organization. Certain very small departments must be consolidated into larger administrative entities. This should be accomplished with an eye to the imperatives of the new program."* Although the statement is not specific, the foreign languages were some of the smaller departments on campus, and one possible interpretation of this proposed change is that the language departments should lose individual departmental status and become components of a larger language department or units of the Cultures of Europe Program.

Along with moving administrative functions to larger units, the grant proposed that "curricular planning and development be interdepartmental and institutional to avoid further decreases in enrollment and imbalance in the distribution of faculty positions." It would seem entirely reasonable that members of small departments would perceive that the drafters of the proposal advocated removing the power to define disciplinary courses of study from the individual departments and placing that power in some interdepartmental body, presumably the Cultures of Europe Program.

The objectives of this proposal contain elements of three major types of change efforts: curricular development, faculty development, and organizational development. The addition of a new program, the emphasis on interdisciplinary approaches, and the creation of a new major are characteristic of curricular development. The fact that existing faculty would have to become competent in new areas and "revitalize" their interests in order to teach adequately in that program represents a faculty development component. Finally, the reorganization of departments into larger units and the creation of an interdisciplinary body to oversee curricular matters constitute organizational development. Thus, if enacted, the proposed Cultures of Europe Program would produce significant changes in the college's structure, personnel, and functions.

Episode 6: Language Faculty's Reaction to the Proposal

When details of the submitted proposal became known, the program was widely rejected by the foreign language faculty, as these comments show:

- I am appalled at the lack of language requirement.
- The aims of the program are opposed to the aims of any self-respecting language department.
- The language element is very important. If there is a Cultures of Europe Program without language, it may not accomplish its objectives.
- I had thought it should have been a program which was more language-oriented than the one we saw.
- Language and culture are integral; it's necessary to use language to integrate culture.

In short, a program that did not include the study of language was unacceptable.

As we have seen throughout these episodes, the language departments saw the basic goal of their disciplines as teaching values and culture through the study of language. They analyzed all discussions of change in terms of that goal. They would react favorably only to those courses of action which would increase the likelihood of achieving it. Since the proposed program actually decreased their ability to meet their objective, no one should have been surprised that they rejected the program. Yet, advocates of the program did expect that the program would benefit the language departments and that the languages would ultimately support it. Program advocates saw the failure of language faculty to support the program as an act against their own best interests.

The basis for the different reactions of these two groups lies in the differences in their underlying assumptions. Program advocates (administrators and faculty members on the Drafting Committee) had made an implicit analysis and concluded that foreign language departments could not get enrollment by continuing to teach only, or even primarily, foreign languages; and without enrollment, the departments were not viable. Therefore, advocates reasoned, it would be appropriate that they expand their function in order to survive. This course of action would also be consistent with the administration's goal of preserving the liberal arts component of the institution that foreign language study represented and maximizing its financial viability. But in the view of the language faculty, if they did not maintain the heart of their discipline, the language

disciplines would become indistinguishable from a history department, since they could only teach about foreign culture. For them,
accepting the tenets of the program amounted to giving up the
identity of their discipline.

One of the sources of frustration and confusion surrounding
the efforts to launch a program was insufficient discussion about
these givens. At least part of the reason that such discussions were
rare had to do with the nature of the single-loop actions of both the
language faculty and program advocates. Many of each group's
actions had the unintended effect of decreasing the likelihood of
dealing with basic issues. For example, when the language requirement was eliminated, the language departments carried on their
existing program despite declining enrollment, and they attributed
sinister motives to anyone who attempted to change their strategy.
Although they kept these evaluations private, they used them as the
basis for their subsequent actions. Discussions with program advocates were usually ambiguous and sufficiently abstract that they had
to talk about very few of the important details. Others' attempts to
force them to do things differently were perceived as attempts to
force them out of their discipline, but that very basic and important
perception was never communicated to anyone working on the
proposal. The closest they came was these comments by several
senior faculty:

- Language study is the heart of the humanities.
- A liberal arts education must include language study.
- You can't study Europe without studying the language.

Program advocates saw such reactions as evidence of inflexibility
and interpreted them in light of their own goals. They thought
they had made it clear that there would be no traditional language
requirement in the new program and that the best interests of the
language departments would be served by designing a "pragmatic"
program.

What was axiomatic for one group was blindness or pig-
headedness from the perspective of the other. Because language
faculty and program advocates did not verbalize these basic differences, they could not express their disagreement in any way other than

for one group to say, "the program should be this" and the other to reply, "No, it should not be that, don't you see?" Each side made inferences about the motives and attributes of the individuals who opposed their wishes. The program advocates saw significant segments of the foreign language faculty as unreasonable, threatened, vulnerable, and unwilling to change. Language faculty saw the program advocates as attempting to impose a program on them, ignorant of what Cultures of Europe should be, arbitrary, antihumanistic, and insensitive to requirements of a liberal education. These evaluations were seldom made public and when they were they were made in anger so that their basis could not be discussed.

Though unexamined, these attributions and inferences still had an impact because human beings base their actions on what they infer to be true. When the foreign language departments showed no desire to redefine their function for pragmatic purposes, the administration acted to manage and control the grant process, design an interdepartmental curriculum, and persuade the languages to participate. And though program advocates never even considered trying to force participation, language faculty saw these attempts to persuade as coercion. Drafting the grant without language participation led language faculty to see the Cultures of Europe Program as "an exercise in academic piety" and a "packaging job." They also saw the motivation to apply for the grant as having nothing to do with the languages' disciplinary interests:

- The purpose of the grant was to get money for the institution.
- There was a desire to get money. I don't see the program as a spin-off from any of the departments.
- The deans should have stayed away. The proposal should have come from the faculty. It has a deanly odor.

Since the language faculty never communicated these evaluations to the people writing the proposal, the basic motivations for the program were undiscussable. The faculty assumed that the motives of program supporters were monetary, whereas the drafters of the proposal saw their own motivations as academic and of service to the institution. In fact, after an interim report to faculty and administrators on the views reported in this book, at least one Drafting Committee member found it hard to believe that the language faculty had made such inferences: "I can't see how they can say that after all the grant proposals we received from faculty and all the time we spent in meetings with departments, faculty and students. They must know better."

This misunderstanding is a small example of a cycle that was repeated many times: Program advocates took an action based on their sincere motivation to help the languages and the institution. From that action, the language faculty inferred a different motivation but never tested the inference because one does not accuse others of having self-serving motives. The language faculty then acted as if the inferred motivation were the actual one. Program advocates used their actions (withdrawal from the planning process) as the basis for further unconfirmed inferences (the faculty is defensive, resistant to change) that led to their subsequent action (managing the change process on their own). That management effort then became the beginning of another inference-action cycle. At the end of the three-year grant period, faculty and program advocates were making the same inferences about each other's motives as they had in the initial months of the effort.

Attributional errors have a way of becoming self-fulfilling. After program advocates inferred defensiveness and resistance to change, they may have acted by withholding information and acting unilaterally so as to "get things done." Those actions may then have made the language faculty more resistant and defensive because it had been excluded. In this way, advocates may have helped create or at least accentuate the very attitudes they found objectionable. Naturally, a similar self-fulfilling phenomenon may have occurred on the faculty side of the interaction and helped to perpetuate the cycle.

Actions based on erroneous inferences also tend to escalate error. Each iteration of such cycles is built on and compounds the errors of previous cycles. As events proceeded at Liberal College, small errors multiplied and minor irritations compounded. In an environment of tension individuals tried to act in the interest of harmony and to avoid exacerbating a delicate situation. They became careful not to communicate their irritation and doubly careful not to communicate their private evaluations and inferences. All of these factors served to obscure the errors and reinforce the dynamics that produced them.

Several months after the proposal was submitted, the agency awarded a sizable grant to Liberal College, and it became necessary to implement the proposed program. The dean appointed a Director of the Cultures of Europe Program and an interdepartmental Cultures of Europe Executive Committee for this purpose. Since the sample program submitted in the grant was hypothetical in nature, and since some faculty names were included just for illustrative purposes, it was necessary for the director to get firm participation commitments from faculty. The dean and director phoned those faculty named in the grant and encouraged them to submit course proposals for committee review. Of the twenty-two faculty named in the grant, fewer than half ever offered courses in the program.

Episode 7: Chairpersons' Reactions to Efforts to Staff the Program

The response of some faculty members to this request for participation was vociferous and unexpected. At least two faculty members approached the dean and complained that they were "being forced" into the program and wanted to know if they would have to go along. As the Executive Committee compiled a roster of possible faculty, chairpersons began to resist. One chairperson argued that his faculty should not have to take part because it would mean a loss of part of the teaching time that a given member contributed to the department. Another refused to release faculty because he felt that participation in the Cultures of Europe Program divided the loyalty of faculty members between the program and the department. A third chairperson would only release those faculty who drew the smallest enrollments and were, presumably, the least effective teachers. A fourth refused to release faculty from departmental assignments because he disapproved of the nature and conceptual content of the program.

Chairpersons may also have objected because it would have made their departments vulnerable if the administration subsequently inferred that they could get along with fewer faculty. As competition for resources at the departmental level increased the importance of a "united front" for arguing one's needs, concern over divided faculty loyalty also increased. At least one chairperson was concerned that participation in a program in which curricular decisions were not made at the department level threatened the autonomy of his discipline. Finally, the teaching faculty's commitment to the program seemed low, partly because they had had little say in the design and implementation of the program, and partly because they felt it did not do justice to their disciplines.

Episode 8: Summer Seminars and Faculty Reactions

Despite resistance, the Cultures of Europe Program gained sufficient staff to proceed, and all participating faculty attended a series of summer seminars run by the Program Director and members of the Executive Committee. The primary purpose of the seminars was to give some unity of theme or methodology to the courses, since faculty came from several disciplines. The secondary purpose was to motivate and interest those faculty who had been marginally interested in taking part. One result of these seminars was a statement of a Cultures of Europe methodology intended to guide the design of all courses in the program.

When school began in the fall, the committee introduced the first Cultures of Europe Program courses. (Eventually, almost twenty such courses were offered.) Student response was disappointing. The introductory course drew fair enrollment when first offered but attrition initially was 30 percent. Over time the attrition rate dropped, but so did enrollment. Many courses were taught with twelve or fewer students, and one course was cancelled because of insufficient enrollment. Some courses drew twenty to thirty students, but at least one of these was discontinued after the instructor blatantly ignored what the Executive Committee told him the course should contain. At the end of the first year, 104 students had enrolled in Cultures of Europe Program courses. At the end of the second year, that number had fallen to eighty.

Because the language departments did not see that the program filled any of their needs, it is not surprising that most of their faculty saw little reason to participate. Those few who participated did so because of perceived pressure and cajoling from the dean. It should also not be surprising that they resisted efforts to establish an interdepartmental body (Cultures of Europe Executive Committee) for review of curricular offerings. (While interviews provided no data directly relevant to this point it is possible that the Executive Committee was seen as an effort to integrate departments under the program in a way consistent with the organizational changes described in the grant proposal.)

From a theory-of-action perspective, foreign language faculty faced a dilemma. On the one hand, if they took part in a program in which the curriculum was controlled by an interdisciplinary group, then, to the extent that the program was successful, they would be teaching a discipline that was defined by someone else, that had a curriculum not under their control, and that seemed intended to eliminate their own discipline. The success of the program would weaken their departments. On the other hand, if they did not participate, they would not receive the help they needed to keep their own department staffed at its current levels. To maintain their disciplines, language faculty would have to take part in a program perceived as inimical to them.

Since neither program advocates nor faculty could influence each other, each acted to achieve its own objectives. Thus, the proposal was written without a language requirement and with the hope that the foreign languages would "get aboard," once the money was available. To maximize the likelihood of winning the grant, it had been necessary to minimize the existing reluctance of the language faculty and to write as if there was internal commitment to the program. To gain financial support, the language faculty publicly went along with the program; a few members even participated, but they privately maintained that they were not doing anything differently:

- This hasn't changed my interests.
- The course in Cultures of Europe is not all that removed from what I was doing.
- The Cultures of Europe Program hasn't affected the way I teach.
- The college is serving as patron to the participating faculty by allowing them to pursue various interests of their own.

So while the program espoused one type of course, faculty actually taught courses which were, by their own description, quite different.

They participated but did not comply with the methodological perspective required. And all the while they made it clear that they did not take part because of their own interests, but because of pressure, persuasion, and cajoling. Several of the language faculty indicated that they would not continue in the program after they had offered their Cultures of Europe course once and accepted the attached $2000 stipend.

Essentially, these faculty were able to ignore the program guidelines and do what they wanted within the program at the same time that they demonstrated some foreign language presence. They taught in a way that was consistent with their current approach and contrary to the intent of the program. They complied with the pressures to participate, but in such a way that the aims of the program were not achieved. Naturally, this noncompliance could be neither blatantly evident nor publicly acknowledged. The result was the creation of a situation in which two groups, out of the highest motives, begin to play games with one another. Faculty repeatedly covered up the fact that they did not share the program advocates' commitment to the Cultures of Europe Program. Unfortunately human beings cannot repeatedly cover up without digging deeper holes for themselves: not only did they play games, they then had to camouflage the games so that they did not become public.

Episode 9: Program Advocates' Reactions to Problems with the Program

Few people in an institution are blind to gamesmanship for long. Members of the committee were aware of these games after seeing the courses faculty actually offered in the program: "We arrived at a situation where they didn't want to do what was required."

The administration and the Executive Committee played their own games. They knew some faculty were teaching poorly or inconsistently with the guidelines, but did not give them the feedback that might have led to improvement. While program administrators disagreed, faculty report being cajoled into participation and then finding that administrators talked about "broad-based response" to the program. The committee said they knowingly took a few faculty who were inadequate teachers in their own disciplines and yet expected them to be an asset to the program. They provided release time with healthy stipends but required little in return. Coupled with this was a norm about interpersonal interactions which ensured that the Director or the Executive Committee was unlikely to confront faculty about inadequate work, and any faculty members asked to leave the program would be unlikely to hear the real reasons. "Someday," according to one committee member, "the committee is going to have to sit down with the faculty members we know are bad and have a discussion and tell them, carefully choosing their words and softening what they say, that we don't want them to teach in the program any more."

The Executive Committee was clearly unwilling to frankly discuss the teachers' competence. This unwillingness to discuss issues that might produce negative feelings prevented faculty members from having to deal with the consequences of their own actions. Because they were already perceived as vulnerable, people made certain that causes other than inadequate performance or lack of professional competence were discussed as the reasons for any shortfall in the program goals. The basic problems of this program, consequently, were not discussed, and therefore were not subject to change.

The real sources of difficulty with the program became hidden beneath an elaborate set of espoused reasons for the action taken by both sides. The espoused causes of problems were the focus of discussion and subsequent action, and they may in fact have been part of the cause, but they were stated in sufficiently ambiguous terms that their precise nature was obscured and the source of the problems could not be isolated, confronted, or altered. In interviews two and one half years after the beginning of the program, program advocates attributed the difficulties of the program to such things as the political-contextual environment; apprehension about steady-state staffing policies; inadequate advertising to students; the difficulty of phasing in an interdisciplinary program; and playing the numbers game. In contrast, the analyses presented in this chapter and in Chapter Four suggest other sources: the languages' unalterable resistance to a nonlanguage program, their fear about losing their disciplinary focus if they were absorbed into the Cultures of

Europe Program, and the departments' withholding of staff support or assigning staff who were unable or unwilling to do a good job.

Any effort to improve the program would fail if it focused on the espoused difficulties and ignored the more important, but less discussable ones identified here. Effective change requires some method of helping individuals discover and/or sort out for themselves the real problems from the espoused ones.

Episode 10: Follow-up

In the third year of the program, the committee made a series of revisions in the Cultures of Europe Program to accommodate student interests and faculty willingness to teach. It decreased the number of required courses and changed the structure of the program so that the courses in existing departments filled requirements for the Cultures of Europe major. One administrator believed that such changes had the following effect: "Internally, we have a group of strong courses. Some that have been taught will not be offered again. Academically, a stronger, more coherent program is emerging. We have fewer, better courses."

The nature of the changes is important and is described in the document submitted to the college senate for approval: "Cultures of Europe seeks to expose students to a mode of cultural analysis which draws on material from several disciplines, especially history, literature, and art." The language departments' low enrollments, overstaffing, and financial need had been the primary impetus for the program, yet the revised program did not even mention them as an element in the curriculum. The language departments had so strongly resisted participation that they ultimately were dropped from the program. It remains for Chapter Four to evaluate how effective the program was in meeting the objectives set for it.

3

The Theory-of-Action Approach to Development

In the Liberal College case, well-intentioned efforts to adjust to the combination of decreased enrollment and financial pressure failed. Individual and institutional actions produced a variety of errors that quickly became an ongoing part of the institution and made it increasingly difficult to change or even to determine the nature and causes of the basic problems. By the end of the third year of the Cultures of Europe Program so many errors had been made that it was almost impossible to trace the reasons for the failure of the program and the whole development process. This chapter presents a summary of the theory-of-action approach for understanding the kinds of errors that occurred. The concept of theories-in-use is defined and developed through several brief example cases. Chapter Four applies the theory-of-action specifically to the Liberal College case. Although the theory-of-action approach was not derived from or necessarily intended for application to institutions of higher learning, it has proved useful for understanding sources of error in industrial and public service organizations (Argyris and Schön, 1974).

As developed by Argyris and Schön (1974, 1978) the theory-of-action focuses on the causes of personal and organizational ineffectiveness in producing change. It assumes that individuals seek to produce change when they become aware of a mismatch between their image of what should be and what actually is. Effective actions bring the actual situation into line with the desired one, whereas actions that produce a real world no closer to the desired one or even further from it are ineffective. It is also possible for a partial match to have unforeseen consequences that mitigate the effectiveness of the act. For example, a dean might be able to cut a department's spending to match expenditures with resources, but if several valued faculty members resigned in protest, the overall effort would be ineffective. In Argyris and Schön's theory, actions that fail to match actual and desired outcomes represent error. A paradox for human action in general and for effective action in colleges and universities in particular is that human beings never intentionally err, yet efforts to bring about change seem to be filled with errors. Discovering, understanding, and correcting unforeseen or unintended errors are central to a theory-of-action approach. If deans, presidents, and faculty are to address their problems more effectively, they must understand how they can act separately with good intentions and yet produce conflict, exacerbate problems, and generate hostility and mistrust.

The assumption that individuals hold internalized rules that they use to help them analyze and respond to a wide variety of situations is basic to the theory-of-action. It is further assumed that a very few such rules or principles are sufficient to derive the wide variety of observed actions. The cognitive rules used to analyze information and design actions are the ultimate source of ineffectiveness and error. This body of rules constitutes a person's theory-of-action. Effectiveness is best increased by making one's theory-of-action explicit, discovering how it tends to produce error, and learning a new one that corrects the old source of error.

Recent work in cognitive psychology (Nisbett and Wilson, 1977) suggests that, in general, individuals find it extremely difficult to report their cognitive processes accurately. The same is true for their theory-of-action. When asked to describe the principles they use to guide their actions in specific situations, most people reply with what Argyris and Schön call an espoused theory. Their espoused theories often contrast sharply with the theories-of-action inferred from observing their behavior. In other words, if one observes a segment of behavior and infers from it the principles a person must have used to produce it, the *inferred* theory-in-use bears little resemblance to the person's *espoused* theory. The result is pervasive inconsistencies between what people say they do and what they actually do. For example, while many members of an institution publicly pronounce their desire for cooperation and collegiality, in actuality their behavior may be characterized by conflict and power struggles.

One characteristic of a theory-in-use is that people use it so quickly and automatically that their actions merge into an ongoing stream of behavior. Theories-in-use provide freedom from the need to stop and think before acting. Smooth and skillful action indicates that one's theories-in-use have been learned so well that they function at a tacit level (Polanyi, 1958, 1967). On the positive side tacit functioning means that effective action comes easily when one's underlying theory-in-use does not produce errors. On the negative side it means that the detection and correction of error is much more difficult than when the action is consciously and deliberately taken.

Model I Theories-in-Use

The theory-of-action concerns two distinctive theories-in-use: Model I is the theory-in-use that underlies single-loop problem solving; Model II is the theory-in-use that reduces single-loop actions and increases effectiveness. Both models are discussed throughout the rest of this chapter.

Most goal-directed behavior is guided by a theory-in-use that incorporates error and blindness to error. Such behavior is referred to by Argyris and Schön as a Model I theory-in-use. While Model I theories-in-use may produce effective action in some circumstances, they also create an inability to deal with problems that require altering the governing values and behavioral strategies of one's tacitly held theory. Governing values are the internal standards against which one judges the acceptability of events. When individuals detect a mismatch between these standards and events they act to alter the situation. Behavioral strategies are general forms that actions take to produce the changes necessary for creating a match.

A simple example may be useful. As part of a larger project, faculty members were interviewed about their teaching and their classroom lectures were observed and recorded. When asked to describe the principles or theory-in-use that guided her teaching, one professor replied that she always tried to make sure students understood one point before going on to the next and that she treated her students with patience and concern. This description constituted her espoused theory. During her lecture, however, very few students raised their hands to ask questions, and those who did were not called on. After the lecture, the professor was asked if she saw any discrepancy between her espoused goal of making certain that students understood the material and her reluctance to call on students with questions. While surprised by her own actions, she saw the inconsistency and vowed to change that aspect of her lecture style. In the next lecture, she did, indeed, call on students with questions. To one student she replied, "That's a very interesting point. Why don't you see me after class to discuss it?" To another who had indicated that he did not understand the point being made, she said, "If this isn't clear, why don't you see me during my office hours?" When asked, this professor indicated that she felt she had made significant changes in her actions.

Did anything important really happen? The professor produced three distinct responses to student questions: ignore them; "see me after class"; and "see me during my office hours." While the specifics of these replies differ, the meaning they communicate is the same: "I do not answer questions in class." From this meaning, it is possible to infer that the different specific actions reflect a single behavioral strategy by which this professor acts to control the class, minimize interruptions, and devote as much time as possible to lecturing. As a result, she is almost always able to cover her prepared material. From her actions and their consequences, one could infer that a goal of her theory-in-use is "Cover all the material for each lecture."

The professor's actions represented a match between her actual behavior and the theory-in-use inferred by the observer, but a mismatch with regard to her espoused goals. This example suggests that individuals can be unaware of incongruities between their espoused and in-use theories. When that incongruity is pointed out and acknowledged, it is easy to produce changes in specific actions, but hard to alter the meaning inherent in them because the only "rules" individuals have for designing their action are the ones they have always used. Because the rules are applied automatically and at a tacit level, they are hard to recognize and hard to change. (An interesting phenomenon is the fact that people tend to be blind to their own inability to change their theories-in-use, but are quite aware of others' difficulty in doing so.)

With this example as background, the theory-of-action approach hypothesizes that most goal-directed human actions can be understood in terms of the four governing values of Model I:

1. *Define your goals and try to achieve them.* Individuals typically define their goals by analyzing situations privately. They seldom change goals, once set, to make them more congruent with the goals of others, and all action is oriented toward meeting those goals.

2. *Maximize winning and minimize losing.* Individuals design actions to increase the likelihood of attaining their goals. They block the actions of others that are incompatible with their desires, ignore information and possible actions not useful for meeting their goals, and select or reinterpret other information in terms of their needs.

3. *Minimize generating and expressing negative feelings.* In general, people are unwilling to make others or themselves angry or upset, so they avoid acting in ways that might produce such reactions. Normally this behavior is valuable because it keeps social relationships running smoothly; but it also leads people to withhold valid information about others' performance or their own reactions when that information might create negative feelings.

4. *Be rational.* Our culture values logic, consistency, and careful reasoning; illogical preferences and/or biases are considered irrelevant or counterproductive in decision making and problem

solving. Therefore people try to keep discussions of issues objective and avoid emotional or personalistic reactions.

Four behavioral strategies associated with Model I produce specific actions and satisfy the governing values:

1. *Design and manage the environment unilaterally.* Individuals make their own analysis of a situation and plan what should be done in private. To get things done their way, they must recruit, persuade, or cajole others.

2. *Own and control the task.* To the extent that individuals can define and control a task through power or persuasion, they can guarantee outcomes consistent with their own goals. Task ownership is both a prerogative of status and a demonstration of power.

3. *Unilaterally protect yourself.* Ambiguity, secrecy, scapegoating, and cover-your-ass behaviors fall under this strategy; they help maintain an advantage and limit vulnerability.

4. *Unilaterally protect others from being hurt.* Because people normally do not wish to hurt another, they sometimes withhold and distort information, do not express anger or disappointment, and tell others what they want to hear. Many of these actions are based on the untested assumption that others are brittle, easily hurt, and unable to use valid information productively if it also produces hurt feelings.

Consequences of Model I Theories-in-Use. This work focuses on processes that inhibit or facilitate effective action. I have taken the position that one uses a theory-in-use to design behavior and that the Model I theory-in-use described above is the prototypical model for designing goal-directed actions. Acting in accord with the behavioral strategies of a Model I theory-in-use means that one will tend to act unilaterally in dealing with others and protectively toward oneself. Success, according to this model, means controlling and influencing others and preventing others from influencing oneself. The use of these strategies leads to mistrusting others, viewing others as uninfluenceable and inflexible, and defending oneself from manipulation so that group and interpersonal relations become more concerned with protecting oneself from others than with facilitating effective problem solving.

Self-Sealing Nature of Model I Actions. The continued interaction between the person trying to impose control and others trying to prevent it creates a self-reinforcing or self-sealing cycle: As one increases efforts to control, the others increase their resistance. Everyone withholds information, distorts his perceptions of others, and is generally distrustful of and unresponsive to feedback. Together, these actions and attitudes reduce the ability of the institution to examine its underlying assumptions and engage in double-loop learning (Argyris and Schön, 1978, pp. 64–65).

Effects of Attributions, Inferences, and Evaluations. To deal effectively with the vast amount of information presented in interpersonal or organizational actions, people must select what is most relevant to their own objectives and summarize it as cogently as possible. They develop the ability to ignore "useless" information and to reinterpret events in terms of their own theories-in-use. For example, if a dean and a chairperson spend several hours discussing the future needs of a particular department, and if the dean argues that funding is not available because other departments are in greater immediate need, the chairperson may describe the dean's position to the faculty as inflexible, unreasonable, or anti-intellectual. The chairperson passes along to others whatever errors he made in forming the abstraction since it is his only summary of the interaction. Such abstractions are useful when they are accurate. But they are always potential sources of error since two people in the same situation may abstract different implications from it. It is possible that the dean in this example felt she had been understanding and conciliatory rather than stubborn and uninformed. The chairperson's failure to illustrate his inferences, attributions, and evaluations with examples from the original interaction makes any errors undetectable and uncorrectable. Typically, Model I behavioral strategies discourage such illustrations. Since people design their future actions on the basis of the analyses embodied in their abstractions, their actions both perpetuate errors and lead to future misunderstandings.

An Example of Model I Processes

The following case, taken from an unpublished account written by the dean of a large university as an example of an interaction in which he felt he had been particularly effective, illustrates the concepts of the theory and their utility. It begins with the dean's brief statement of the problem confronting him and his description of his goals and strategy. It then splits into two columns: In one the dean reports the dialogue that actually occurred between himself and department chairpersons, and in the other he reports his thoughts at the time. Thus, the right-hand column consists of what was publicly said and the left-hand one the dean's private reactions.

The dean writes: "The situation involves an interaction between myself [the dean] and two department chairmen, A and B. Important economies at the university can and must be made, primarily by inducing A and B to coordinate their programs, reduce the number of low-enrollment courses, coordinate sabbatical leaves, develop joint programs, and coordinate course sequences to maximize flexibility for students. If one or both departments are subsequently forced to reduce faculty for economic reasons, it will be possible to reduce the negative effects through this cooperation.

"Thus far, cooperation has been on the basis of convenience. There has not been a sharp focus on steps that would provide specific economies or reduce costs. If cooperation is to become significant, it must be evident that important economies can be achieved and certain costs to each department reduced. The university has provided funds to develop such cooperative programs. I have called a meeting of the two chairmen to encourage their departments (which are in different schools in the university) to discuss possibilities for closer cooperation that would benefit the university, departments, and students. My strategy is to (1) reduce the threat to cooperation, (2) reinforce ideas or suggestions for cooperation, and (3) provide examples of how other departments have cooperated to achieve the university's goals."

Underlying Thoughts

Dialogue

This meeting wouldn't have been necessary if the chairmen of these

Dean: Thank you for coming to this meeting to discuss the possibilities

Underlying Thoughts

Dialogue

two departments had taken their own initiative to plan jointly as was requested of all department chairpersons. I have been annoyed at their lack of cooperation.

Chairman A would like to keep things just as they are and get me off his back. He knows full well that he hasn't really tried to promote cooperation, and Chairman B is the same. Chairman B also feels that his program is superior to the one offered in Department A.

for cooperation between your two departments. I have been looking forward to this meeting for us to jointly examine some of the possibilities for closer cooperation.

Chairman A: As you probably know, Dean, we have been cooperating under this joint program in that the students do cross-register in some of our courses. We've had a few students from Department B come over here and some of our students have gone over to Department B for courses.

Dean: This is very good! Do you think cross-registrations in your department will increase?

Chairman B: We have permitted students to cross-register as long as they meet the requirements for the courses in which they are enrolling. However, it is very difficult for some of Department A's students to meet the prerequisites for many of our courses, especially upper-level courses. Our departments are very different, and there probably won't be much cross-registration.

Because of changes in personnel in Department A, this is a perfect time for these two departments to consider closer cooperation.

Dean: As you know, two faculty in Department A are not returning next year. The year after next, a third member of A will be retiring. This is an opportune time for your two departments to do some planning, perhaps by using a model in which you imagine that you are one department serving the campus. How would a single department with your combined faculty members serve the student population? I believe that this is the question we need to examine today.

Underlying Thoughts

Dialogue

Chairman A is willing to consider cooperation because he has identified a specific need. Chairman B, however, is likely to feel that Department A will reap all the benefits.

Chairman A: One area where we could cooperate would be if Chairman B were willing to teach his specialty to our students.

I should try to reinforce any suggestion for cooperation.

Dean: That's a good example for the possibility of productive cooperation, Chairman A.

I know Chairman B is determined not to cooperate on this matter, but at least I will try to counter some of the points that he has made.

Chairman B: I should make it very clear from the start that I personally would not be willing to teach a course in Department A. I was appointed to teach in Department B and believe it would be unproductive for me to split my time between the two departments.

Dean: Other faculty members who have been involved have tried to overcome the problems of splitting time. Some have reduced their course preparation by teaching one section of the same course in each department. Students and faculty alike have reported to me that this is not as wasteful of their time as one might at first imagine.

Chairman B: If we cooperate too closely our two departments will become identical, and frankly I'm not willing to change our program because I think we have an excellent program. Furthermore, students in Department B aren't going to want to have to take courses in Department A in order to complete a major. If we begin to force our students to take courses in other departments, it will be a disservice to them. We may, in fact, lose some of our good students because they won't put up with the hassle.

Chairman A: I agree with Chair-

Underlying Thoughts

Dialogue

Chairman A: I agree with Chairman B that if we begin to require students to take courses in other departments we might, in fact, begin to turn them away from our programs. I would not want our programs to be seen as identical because, as Chairman B has stated, this would reduce our ability to attract students to our home departments.

These responses reflect fears that are common among many faculty. These fears are based more on fiction than on fact. To reduce these fears I should provide real examples and point out that in some areas we don't have any evidence to go on.

Dean: The evidence that we have so far is that cross-registration between departments in different schools is becoming more popular with students. Students have been very, very pleased with the opportunity to take courses in other schools. With regard to becoming identical, are there things that you would like to do for your students that you cannot now because you don't have enough personnel? Are there ways to identify each department with specific areas in the discipline to reduce the problem of being seen as the same? By joint planning, Department Z has been able to offer a program which it was not able to offer previously because of personnel shortages.

   If departments creatively plan together they can better serve their students and better use their personnel at no additional cost to the university. Through improved programming in the academic departments, we will strengthen both programs and be more attractive to students so that we will have a much brighter and healthier future.

The chairmen must now develop specific ideas for cooperation that we can examine at a specified date in

   What I would like the two of you to do in the next four weeks is to try out some different models of

Underlying Thoughts	*Dialogue*
the near future. The burden must now be placed with them. If they carry out their mandate, it will be an important step in reducing their resistance to cooperation and will open up possibilities they were not able to see previously. I am sure this task will require great effort on their part.	a joint program. I would like to have at least one, possibly two or three, fairly complete models of course offerings at the two departments. If you would like me to join you in these discussions, I am open to your invitation. Do you have any questions? Thank you so much for coming. I'm looking forward to the possibilities for cooperation that you will be developing in the next four weeks.

This case is a microcosm of many situations existing in higher education. The institution, like so many others, faces strong financial pressures. In analyzing the effects of these pressures on the institution, the dean has made his goal the reduction of costs. Once this goal is established, Model I behavioral strategies are engaged to ensure that the goal is attained. His selection and processing of information about the institution have been pervasively affected; that is, he has selectively sought situations that offer or can be made to offer cost reduction opportunities. He sees factors arguing against reductions as obstacles to be overcome rather than as justifiable impediments to cutting costs. All of his actions have been designed to control the situation and persuade individuals to accept his interpretation of the problem and the solution. While these strategies might produce the greatest financial savings, the accompanying selection and interpretation of information increases the likelihood of reaching conclusions or taking actions that individuals affected by the cuts will see as erroneous or ill advised. Actions that create a match between the dean's goals and the environment simultaneously create a mismatch for the chairmen, who design their subsequent actions to "correct" the situation.

The tacit nature of each side's analysis and the role of each theory-in-use in biasing information have several consequences that escalate the conflict and reduce everyone's effectiveness. The dean has arrived at a number of inferences and evaluations that become the basis for his course of action. He has concluded (1) that two departments are similar enough to be integrated, (2) that what is good for the financial health of the institution is good for the departments, (3) that the loss of three faculty makes this a particularly good time to make further changes, and (4) that reasonable people must see the situation as he does. All of these conclusions are consistent with his objectives in that if they are correct, there is a clear-cut way to reduce costs. Furthermore, labeling objections as unreasonable helps to specify the appropriate strategy for meeting his objectives: namely, focus on persuading the chairmen that their objections are not valid. If they cannot see on their own that cooperation makes sense, it is reasonable for the dean to use his power to order the "right" changes.

At the same time, several characteristics of the dean's theory-in-use make his analysis undiscussable. In part, the tacit nature of the analysis itself makes discussion of these conclusions unlikely, especially when combined with Model I governing values and behavioral strategies, which keep discussions vague and evaluations unillustrated. For example, if the dean avoids specifics about the evaluation that formed the basis of his actions, he can control discussions by focusing only on reasoning consistent with the actions. If he were to make his evaluation public, he would be vulnerable to counter argument and would have to deal with information he had previously seen as unimportant or topics that others were better informed about than he. His inference about the similarity of the two departments would be especially vulnerable to counter argument by the experts in the respective areas. Discussion of that point would decrease his control of the situation and lessen his chances of producing change.

Part of the motivation that underlies the dean's behavior may be avoiding negative reactions from A and B—one of the governing values of Model I. For example, if budgets and/or staffing are reduced, the chairmen may believe they will lose their departmental identities. Eliminating low-enrollment courses may mean removing seminars from the curriculum. Both losses certainly would be upsetting to the chairmen and their faculty. While these losses may be necessary if the dean is to attain his goal, it becomes natural for him to try to soften the blow by being ambiguous, talking in generalities about cooperation and the best use of faculty, and discussing hypothetical situations.

The dean's ambiguity is very likely to produce a dysfunctional response vis-à-vis his objectives. It may produce a cycle wherein (1) the dean seeks cooperation by first trying to reason with A and B, (2) he tries harder to persuade them when he sees that they don't share his reasoning and oppose his goals, (3) A and B look for ways to meet their own goals, not his (assuming for the moment that their goal is to maintain the strength and autonomy of their departments), and (4) the dean interprets their actions as further examples of being uncooperative and orders them to do as he wishes. The dean's own actions have then helped create the behavioral world he finds so upsetting.

The combination of the dean's theory-in-use and the tacit nature of his analyses conspired to prevent discussion or alteration of the basis for his actions. The undiscussability of his inferences ensured that any errors in them would go undetected. A and B may have been perfectly willing to cooperate with one another. The difficulty may have been that A and B would cooperate toward goals that were not compatible with the dean's. Had the dean stated his evaluations, he might have learned of that willingness and have come closer to the heart of the conflict between his goals and those of A and B.

The resulting pattern of attempts to persuade or cajole followed by resistance to persuasion became self-sealing and was maintained by Model I theories-in-use, which are highly resistant to change. The only way to alter such a pattern is to test or discuss the inferences, goals, and theory-in-use that underlie it. Yet the governing values and behavioral strategies of Model I make it unlikely that one would risk public testing and the loss of unilateral control entailed in uncovering one's analyses, assumptions, and theories-in-use. Model I theories-in-use therefore perpetuate single-loop learning and self-sealing interpersonal and group processes. Even the application of power in this case does not mean an end to self-sealing activities. Despite the dean's order to cooperate, A and B might well get together and try to minimize their losses by resisting course and staffing changes in their departments whenever possible. The self-sealing cycle produced by the interaction of the dean's and the chairmen's theories-in-use is likely to become part of the behavioral world of the university and to increase conflict, decrease morale, and consume both faculty and administrative time and energy. This cycle and some of its components are schematically represented in Figure 1.

Inconsistencies Between Espoused and In-Use Theories. The need to make public appeals in terms acceptable to those with differing objectives, and the need to act in ways that achieve one's own objectives produce inconsistencies between what is said and what is done or between espoused theory and theory-in-use. It may be possible to get support for a time by calling on norms of collegiality or purporting to "further the needs of the university," but failing to act in ways others can see as meeting those needs eventually makes the inconsistencies apparent. However, these inconsistencies are seldom publicly confronted because confrontations would create negative feelings and because people tend to assume that the inconsistencies they see are also obvious to those who create them. For example, the espoused impetus for the dean's effort was to benefit the institution, faculty, departments, and students. Yet the chairmen could hardly see losing faculty and curricular offerings as beneficial. Likewise, the dean had listed the reduction of threat to faculty as one of his goals, yet talk of combining departments and losing staff was a great threat to faculty.

The fact that people act in ways different from what they espouse is not inherently detrimental to institutional functioning. Inconsistency is a natural product of complexity and is neither positive nor negative per se. Some inconsistencies are benign whereas others are indicative of counterproductive group processes. Where conflict and/or inability to solve organizational problems exist, looking into inconsistencies can help lead to the root issues that are always embedded in individuals' goals, assumptions, and theories-in-use. For such discoveries to occur, the behavioral environment must encourage double-loop learning and explicit statement of and inquiry into organizational inconsistencies.

In the case of this university, the dean and the chairmen are both trying to achieve what they sincerely believe to be best for the institution, yet their interaction has set the stage for a long series of events characterized by tension, conflict, and mistrust. When members of an institution share Model I theories-in-use, as the dean and his chairmen do, the governing values and behavioral strategies

Figure 1. Self-sealing Processes.

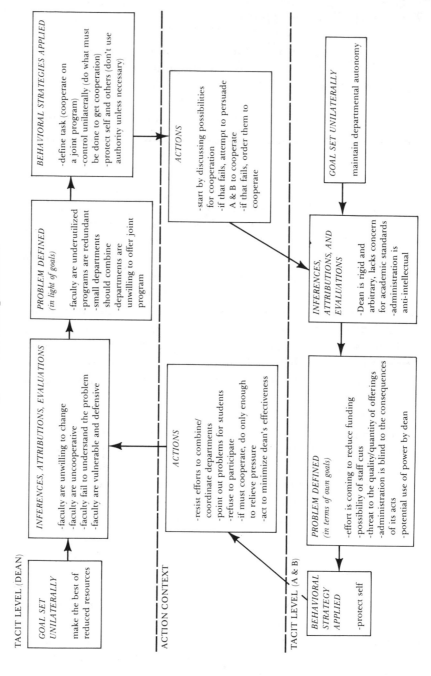

TACIT LEVEL (DEAN)

GOAL SET UNILATERALLY

make the best of reduced resources

INFERENCES, ATTRIBUTIONS, EVALUATIONS

- faculty are unwilling to change
- faculty are uncooperative
- faculty fail to understand the problem
- faculty are vulnerable and defensive

PROBLEM DEFINED
(in light of goals)

- faculty are underutilized
- programs are redundant
- small departments should combine
- departments are unwilling to offer joint program

BEHAVIORAL STRATEGIES APPLIED

- define task (cooperate on a joint program)
- control unilaterally (do what must be done to get cooperation)
- protect self and others (don't use authority unless necessary)

ACTION CONTEXT

ACTIONS

- resist efforts to combine/coordinate departments
- point out problems for students
- refuse to participate
- if must cooperate, do only enough to relieve pressure
- act to minimize dean's effectiveness

ACTIONS

- start by discussing possibilities for cooperation
- if that fails, attempt to persuade A & B to cooperate
- if that fails, order them to cooperate

TACIT LEVEL (A & B)

BEHAVIORAL STRATEGY APPLIED

- protect self

PROBLEM DEFINED
(in terms of own goals)

- effort is coming to reduce funding
- possibility of staff cuts
- threat to the quality/quantity of offerings
- administration is blind to the consequences of its acts
- potential use of power by dean

INFERENCES, ATTRIBUTIONS, AND EVALUATIONS

- Dean is rigid and arbitrary, lacks concern for academic standards
- administration is anti-intellectual

GOAL SET UNILATERALLY

maintain departmental autonomy

become embedded in the organizational environment and compound the sources of error existing at the individual level.

The institutional theory-in-use puts emphasis on politics, persuasion, and power as methods of producing change and contains forces that keep important information scattered, ambiguous, and inaccessible. As a consequence, the institution's efforts at problem solving are largely single loop in nature. Double-loop change—a Model II theory-in-use—is difficult and painful because important assumptions and goals are usually accessible only in times of institutional distress. The trauma of crisis is necessary to mobilize the willingness and effort necessary to produce change.

Model II Theory-in-Use

The theoretical position taken here suggests that most attempts to solve problems are governed by Model I theories-in-use, which facilitate single-loop learning but create blindness to sources of error related to double-loop problems. As the preceding discussion has shown, individuals are highly unlikely to detect and correct problems affected by their unspoken values and assumptions when the behavioral world they have created functions with Model I theories-in-use. The creation of a behavioral world that encourages inquiry into theories-in-use, leads to public testing of analyses and assumptions, and does not rely on strategies of unilateral control to achieve one's objectives is essential to discovering the errors embedded in one's tacit processes. Such a world and such skills must be based on or informed by a different theory-of-action. Argyris and Schön (1978, pp. 136–139) concisely describe such an alternative theory-of-action, Model II:

> Briefly, the governing variables or values of Model II are not the opposite of Model I. The governing variables are: valid information, free and informed choice, and internal commitment [Table 1].
> The behavior required to fulfill these values also is not the opposite of Model I. For example, Model I emphasizes that the individuals be as articulate as they can be about their purposes and simultaneously control the others and the environment in order to ensure that their purposes are achieved. Model

II does not reject the skill or competence to be articulate and precise about one's purposes. It does reject the unilateral control that usually accompanies advocacy because the typical purpose of advocacy is to win. Model II couples articulateness and advocacy with an invitation to others to confront one's views, to alter them in order to produce the position that is based on the most complete valid information possible and to which people involved can become internally committed. This means the actor (in Model II) is skilled at inviting double-loop learning on the part of other individuals. . . .

The behavioral strategies of Model II involve sharing power with anyone who has competence and who is relevant to deciding or implementing the action. The definition of the task and the control over the environment are now shared with all the relevant actors. Saving one's own face or that of others is resisted because it is seen as a defensive nonlearning activity. . . .

Under these conditions individuals will not tend to compete to make decisions for others, to one-up others, or to outshine others for the purposes of self-gratification. Individuals in a Model II world seek to find the most competent people for the decision to be made. They seek to build viable decision-making networks in which the major function of the group is to maximize the contributions of each member so that when a synthesis is developed, the widest possible exploration of views has occurred.

Finally, if new concepts are created under Model II conditions, the meaning given to them by the creator and the inference processes used to develop them are open to scrutiny by those who are expected to use them. Evaluations and attributions are minimized. However, when they are used, they are coupled with the directly observable data which lead to the formation of the evaluation or attribution. Also, the creator feels responsible for presenting the evaluations and attributions in ways that encourage their open and constructive confrontation. . . .

The consequence for learning should be an emphasis on double-loop learning, by means of which individuals confront the basic assumptions behind the present views of others and invite confrontation of their own basic assumptions, and by which where underlying hypotheses are tested publicly and are made disconfirmable, not self-sealing. Where individuals function as agents of organizational learning, the consequences of Model II should be an enhancement of the conditions for *organizational* double-loop learning, where assumptions and norms central to organizational theory-in-use are surfaced, publicly confronted, tested, and restructured.

Table 1. Model II

Governing values	Behavioral strategies for actor and toward environment	Consequences for behavioral world	Consequences for learning
Valid information Free and informed choice Internal commitment to the choice and constant monitoring of the implementations	Design situations or encounters where participants can be originators and experience high personal causation Task is controlled jointly Protection of self is a joint enterprise and oriented toward growth Bilateral protection of others	Actor experienced as minimally defensive Minimally defensive interpersonal relations and group dynamics Learning-oriented norms High freedom of choice, internal commitment, and risk taking	Disconfirmable, not self-sealing hypotheses Double-loop learning Frequent testing of theories by stating inferences, evaluations, attributions to see whether others agree

Source: Based on Argyris and Schön (1978).

The spirit of this model is doubtlessly familiar and widely valued. In some ways it incorporates many pervading societal values. Interestingly enough, even though learners may value a Model II theory-of-action, intellectually understand it, and espouse a strong desire to master it, they are often distressed to find it very difficult to design actions that are consistent with it. They do not seem to be able to make it their theory-in-use, and they are unaware of their inability to do so (Argyris and Schön, 1978, p. 139). At the same time, other individuals with whom they attempt to practice producing Model II behavior are immediately aware of their failure.

The result is frustration for the persons involved, and is a primary problem to be solved: How does one change one's theory-in-use? Chapter Four illustrates how Model I can be used to clearly define underlying problems and to specify the focus for needed change; the central topic of Chapter Five is one group's attempts to do this.

4

Analyzing Sources
of Ineffectiveness

This chapter is an effort to fit the theory-of-action model to the case presented in Chapter Two and to determine its usefulness for discovering the roots of Liberal College's failure to produce change or solve its original problems. The most important point of the chapter is to show how a theory-of-action analysis produces insights into the dynamics of the interaction between program advocates and faculty. If such an analysis can make that understandable, the first step toward understanding how to produce change will have been taken.

The single-loop nature of both faculty and program advocates' action is best understood when the goals inherent in each group's theory-in-use are clear. Program advocates had unilaterally set their goal: Improve the institution by providing an attractive, enthusiastically supported nonlanguage curriculum. This goal became part of their theory-in-use and was neither discussable nor alterable, yet it had a pervasive effect on their analysis of and reaction to the language faculty. For example, their original request to the language faculty for a grant proposal was based on the assumption that language faculty shared the program advocates' goal and would design a nonlanguage program; naturally they saw the language study program the faculty suggested as a mismatch. Their subsequent actions focused on this mismatch and away from examining their own or the faculty's goals and assumptions. Instead of discovering that different goals existed, advocates made sense of the initial proposal by inferring that language faculty misunderstood the granting agency's requirements. They also inferred that the faculty knew they could not continue with their current heavy emphasis on language. Since neither of these inferences was discussed with members of the language faculty, the inherent error was undetectable and hence uncorrectable. The program advocates tried to solve the problem (i.e., replace the mismatch with a match) by correcting the *inferred* source of error. They explained that language study was unacceptable and tried to persuade the language faculty to rewrite the proposal within the guidelines. The language departments withdrew from the grant effort altogether rather than comply with the non–language study guideline.

The events to this point represent one iteration of a single-loop learning cycle. It is single loop because the advocates' theory-in-use that produced the first error (language departments' failure to comply) also produced the second error (language departments' withdrawal from the effort) and because there was no effort to test whether their own theory-in-use might have been the source of error. The language departments' withdrawal presented advocates with another mismatch and led to another inference—namely that the language departments were defensive and resistant to change—and so the single-loop cycle continued. At the same time, faculty produced their own single-loop solutions to the mismatches created for them by the advocates' actions. Their unilaterally set goal of maintaining their discipline and curriculum led them to attempt to block any change. They, too, followed the cycle of detecting a mismatch vis-à-vis their goals, making inferences, failing to test the inferences, and basing their actions on them. Their resulting action produced another problem for advocates and was the basis for advocates' subsequent actions.

All these single-loop solutions were maintained and perpetuated by Model I theories-in-use. Some of the major iterations of these loops are presented in Table 2. As the table shows, the actions of both groups shared the same distinguishing characteristics: untested inferences and evaluations; undiscussable, unilaterally set goals; efforts to create an environment that matched these goals; and failure to detect the source of error because of inability to examine and change governing values and behavioral strategies. Notice too that each group's inferences and actions make good sense and appear rational from the perspective of their own goals and theories-in-use. The table also makes it apparent that errors are compounded at each step. At the beginning, errors come from fairly direct attempts to deal with the problems created by others' actions. By the end, actions are designed to hide previous errors or to disguise the reasons for hiding errors. Thus Model I theories-in-use do not create single problems but introduce escalating problems and create obstacles.

What is the role of power in this sequence of events? Program advocates, who had the backing of the administration, could unilaterally do what they felt necessary, whereas the foreign language faculty, having no comparable power, could either cooperate or refuse participation and privately adhere to their own objectives. In the end, however, power made no difference, because to make the program successful, advocates would have had to change faculty members' theories-in-use about their discipline. Such changes occur only when individuals freely choose to change and are internally committed to the objectives of the change program. Changing faculty members' theories-in-use was highly unlikely because program advocates used strategies that imposed commitment and minimized the language faculty's choices.

Meanings Behind the Actions

Actions are the raw material from which others infer meanings—meanings that may be discrepant from what was intended. Inferred meanings are important because they form the basis for subsequent action.

So far, two levels of meaning have been considered. The first level consists of the words that individuals say or the actions they take; this is the level of directly observable data. Since these data can

Table 2. Single-loop Solutions

Number of Single-Loop Iterations	Program Advocates		Foreign Language Faculty	
1	*Evaluation:* Language departments cannot survive with current level of enrollment			
	Inference: Must get outside support for language departments in order to cushion a transition in their curriculum	*Action:* Ask languages to draft a proposal for new program	*Inference:* If they want a proposal to save language departments, it means they want a language study program	*Action:* Make proposals for language study
2	*Inference:* Language departments know they can't continue with current emphasis of program			
	Inference: They misunderstood that proposal can't have language requirement	*Action:* Explain that language requirement is unacceptable. Attempt to persuade language faculty to revise proposal	*Evaluation:* A grant without support for language study is irrelevant/useless for us	*Action:* Withdraw interest and support from proposal-planning process
3	*Inference:* Foreign language faculty are defensive and resistant to change, but outside support is essential if they are to survive	*Action:* Appoint committee to draft grant to make use of foreign language faculty in non-language program	*Evaluation:* This kind of program is unacceptable *Attribution:* Advocates are being arbitrary, are seeking money for the college, trying to force us into a program	*Action:* Continued withdrawal, lack of support/co-operation
4	*Evaluation:* This program is essential. Language faculty are persuadable	*Action:* Proposal drafted without language requirement	*Evaluation:* This proposal will not help the languages. It is outside the range of programs acceptable to us	*Action:* Memo to Drafting Committee taking position that requirement for six-semester equivalent of language study should be included in proposal

Table 2. (Continued)

Number of Single-Loop Iterations	Program Advocates		Foreign Language Faculty
5	*Inference:* Languages are reactionary and uncooperative		
	Evaluation: Despite this, we must have outside support for them	*Action:* Final proposal with minimal language requirement	
		(Grant Awarded)	
		Action: Appoint Program Director and Executive Committee	
		Action: Solicit course proposals. Attempt to persuade/cajole faculty to participate	*Inference:* This group is trying to force my participation	*Action:* Some faculty reject the program
				Action: Some faculty complain of coercion to dean
				Action: Other faculty agree with program goals or are persuaded to take part
6	*Evaluation:* We must generate pressure to get support for program	*Action:* Attempt to get chairpersons to release faculty	*Evaluation:* This program is not in the best interest of my department/discipline	*Action:* Refuse to release faculty or only release those with low enrollments. Object to nature of program
7	*Evaluation:* It is necessary to get the faculty committed to the program and to create a unifying framework			
	Evaluation: Departments and faculty do not see the purposes of the program as they should	*Action:* Committee members lead summer seminars to establish policy statement and evolve a "methodology"	*Evaluation:* We cannot agree about the form of the program. These meetings are not useful	*Action:* Attend seminars, but teach course with little regard for methodology or policy statement. Talk as if follow-

Table 2. (Continued)

Number of Single-Loop Iterations	Program Advocates		Foreign Language Faculty	
			ing methods (play games to cover noncompliance)	
8	*Evaluation:* Faculty are not doing what is needed for a good Cultures of Europe Program			
	Inference: Faculty are too vulnerable/brittle to confront with lack of performance	*Action:* Protect faculty by not giving feedback about poor performance, but still try to "bring them around"	*Evaluation:* We've succeeded in upholding our own goals, even while participating in program, but advocates should not know that this was the case	*Action:* Espouse reasons other than real ones for leaving program or for program's failure (camouflage/games)

be recorded and verified by independent observation, they are relatively unambiguous. The second level consists of the interpersonally significant meanings conveyed by the directly observable behavior. For example, consider a dean who only asks people to his office to evaluate their work. If that dean meets a faculty member and says, "Tom, I wonder if you would stop by my office sometime," two levels of meaning are quite clear. The first level is a cordial request, while the second might be paraphrased as "Tom, come to my office. I have some criticisms of your work." Most people are likely to respond to the second meaning.

It is useful now to introduce a third level of meaning: inferences about underlying behavioral strategies. These are based on second-level meanings. The third level brings to bear some of the theoretical notions of Model I and begins to reveal patterns that are inherent in the data but not readily apparent. It is the first step in making explicit the theory-in-use that is embedded in action. The third level of meaning relates specific actions and their inherent meanings to a theoretical framework and thereby gives us a more abstract understanding of the actions and their unintended consequences.

We can examine the actions of both the faculty and the program advocates at Liberal College and see both the meanings of their actions and the behavioral strategies they used. What does the examination reveal? While the specific actions ranged from withdrawing from the proposal planning to taking part in the grant implementation, all actions represent applications of the same behavioral strategy, that is, a strategy for producing an environment acceptable in light of each group's governing values. At the third level of meaning Model I is useful for understanding behavior. Table 3 presents a levels-of-meaning analysis for program advocates and Table 4 a similar analysis for the foreign language departments.

It is worth noting that each group repeatedly tried to define the task in light of its own goals while ignoring the other's definition. When the grant was received the power of money and the administration's endorsement superficially resolved the issue of who would define and control the task; but in actuality, faculty opposition was simply driven into hiding. Because of the bad feelings generated, program advocates felt that they had to protect faculty who had "gone through so much," so they did not talk to the faculty about their weak performance and lack of compliance. Faculty members saved face by overtly subscribing to the program and espousing reasons for the shortcomings of the program that were acceptable to advocates. As a consequence, while the problems existing in the college had been the original focus of their energy, by the end of the grant period most individuals had diverted their energy to face saving and political infighting.

It is instructive, though admittedly artificial, to see the results of putting second-level meanings into a dialogue of what program advocates (PA) and foreign language departments (FL) said to one another through their actions over this period of time. Such a dialogue would go something like this:

PA: Changes need to be made in the foreign languages.
FL: The kind of program we need must include language study.
PA: Language departments need to design a program which shifts away from language study.

Table 3. Program Advocates' Actions Designed to
"Find Financial Support"

Single-loop Cycle	Directly Observable Actions	Inferred Meaning	Underlying Behavioral Strategies
	Increasing level of abstraction ⟶		
1	Ask language departments to propose new program	Changes need to be made in the foreign languages	Define and control task
2	Explain that language requirement is unacceptable. Attempt to persuade language faculty to revise proposal	Language departments need to design a program that shifts away from language study	Define and control task
3	Appoint Drafting Committee without language faculty members to propose a nonlanguage program using foreign language faculty	There will be a program even if the languages don't propose it	Define and control task
4	Proposal made without language requirement	There will be a program regardless of language faculty's resistance	Define and control task
	(Grant Received)		
5	Appoint Program Director and Executive Committee. Solicit course proposals. Persuade/cajole participation	The program will be controlled by a group other than the language departments. The language faculty should get into the program	Define and control task
6	Try to get chairpersons to release faculty	Departments should give up staff so Cultures of Europe can gain staff	Define and control task
7	Committee members lead summer seminar to establish policy statement and evolve a methodology	It is time to formulate guidelines for what these faculty are to do	Define and control task
8	Protect faculty by not giving feedback about poor performance; but still try to bring them around	We know what you are doing, but we won't tell you	Protect self and others

Table 4. Language Faculty's Actions Designed to "Minimize Loss of Disciplinary Integrity and Curricular Autonomy"

Single-loop Cycle	Directly Observable Actions	Inferred Meaning	Underlying Behavioral Strategies
	Increasing level of abstraction ⟶		
1	Make proposal for language study in response to administration's request	The kind of program we need must include language study	Define and control task
2	Withdraw support for drafting process	If we can't design a program to fit our needs, we will have no part of process	Protect selves
3	Continue withdrawal, lack of support/ cooperation	We want no part of existing proposal and without us proposal makes no sense	Define and control task Protect selves
4	Memo stating position that requirement for six-semester equivalent language study should be in proposal (Grant Awarded)	We will tell you the conditions acceptable to us	Define and control task
5	Some faculty reject program. Some faculty complain to dean of coercion. Chairpersons refuse to release faculty and object to nature of program	We do not want this program and will do as little as possible to support it	Protect selves
6	Attend seminar, but teach course with little regard for methodology or policy statement. Speak about course as if following methodology (play games to cover noncompliance)	We will join program, but will do what we want. We will tell you what you want to hear	Define and control task Protect selves
7	Espouse reasons other than real ones for leaving program or for program's failure (camouflage/games)	We have objections to the program, and are going to leave. We'll tell you reasons acceptable to you for our doing this	Protect selves

FL: If we can't design a program to fit our needs, we'll have no part of the process.

PA: There will be a program even if the languages don't propose it.

FL: We want no part of the existing proposal and without us, the program makes no sense.

PA: There will be a program regardless of the language faculty's resistance.

FL: We will tell you the conditions acceptable to us.

(Grant Awarded)

PA: The program will be controlled by a non-language department body, but we'd like the language faculty to get into the program.

FL: We do not want this program and will do as little as possible to support it.

PA: Departments should give up staff so Cultures of Europe can gain staff. It is time to formulate guidelines for what these faculty are to do.

FL: We will go along with the program, but do what we want. We'll tell you what you want to hear.

PA: We know what you are doing, but won't tell you that we know.

FL: We have objections to the program and are going to leave, but we'll espouse reasons acceptable to you for doing this.

Despite its artificiality, this dialogue does help illustrate how the proposal-planning process and the actual grant implementation activity could generate negative, hostile reactions from both faculty and advocates. The interaction was extremely frustrating because each group perceived that it had stated its position and that the other group understood but ignored it. In actuality, each group interpreted what the other said in light of its own theory-in-use and did not detect the differences in meaning each assigned to the same actions.

Consider the kind of behavioral world that Model I theories-in-use create. As we have seen, Model I theories-in-use lead to single-loop behavior and blindness to errors and contradictions. From the perspective of a theory-of-action, individual actions are the basic building blocks for creating the larger social and organizational units in which individuals exist. Since members of an institution share knowledge of how things are done, it is possible to speak of institution-wide rules for action that incorporate individuals' theories-in-use and define the institution's behavioral world. If the individuals began with Model I theories, the behavioral world will incorporate them and reinforce single-loop learning in individuals, departments, and the administration.

At the individual level people make untested inferences, attributions, and evaluations and build their goals and strategies on those bases. They facilitate their own goal achievement by withholding important information and discussing issues ambiguously enough that others may join with them. They attempt to persuade others to share their unilaterally set objectives and act on them. At the department level individuals share goals related to departmental autonomy and power; consequently department members help to keep intradepartmental conflicts private and to present a united front to those outside the department. At the administrative level individual administrators avoid open conflict by working with those faculty members who can be persuaded to share their views. Bad feelings are limited by discussing sensitive issues in private and censoring the justification given for administrative actions. The typical way to get things done is to take an action first, then try to convince the faculty of its necessity. Power is used only when persuasion fails to bring agreement.

What are the consequences of the behavioral world these actions produce? Typically critical information remains scattered and ambiguous; loyalty and diplomacy are emphasized over competence and effectiveness; competition, rivalry, and defensiveness are high; strong departments dominate faculty decision making and put pressure on the administration, so that departments with the greatest needs get the least help; trust and risk-taking are low; and increasing energy gets devoted to politics and conflict management. Overall there is low morale, frustration, and resignation to an inability to change. Individuals become pessimistic about both the possibility of solving the problems confronting them and the capability of the institution to produce any effective change. What change does occur is imposed by the application of power, so that internal commitment is low and cooperation unlikely. Individuals act to protect their existing prerogatives, and departmentalism and power-centered competition become a way of life. All this occurs in an environment in which resistance to change and underlying theories-in-use are undiscussable.

This Model I behavioral world existed prior to the Cultures of Europe effort. From the theory-of-action perspective, the institutional environment and individuals' theories-in-use interacted with and reinforced one another. Both acted to reduce the likelihood that any of the program advocates' changes would be accepted.

Faculty Reactions to the Program and its Objectives

Faculty responses to the program and its objectives are a primary indicator of how successfully the program engaged and changed faculty interests. Faculty evaluations of the program's achievements should be indicators of the program's ability to meet its objectives. The reactions of faculty (both in and out of the language departments) and administrators were collected at two interview sessions, one approximately a year after the grant was awarded and the other after two and one half years of the three-year grant period. All faculty interviewed had prepared and/or taught at least one course in Cultures of Europe. Four members of the Executive Committee were interviewed. The comments of these two sets of individuals are the basis for the following description of the institution's reaction to and acceptance of the Cultures of Europe Program. These reactions are organized around the relevant program objectives: fostering unity, eliminating redundancy and competition, stimulating innovation, and giving relief to departments in greatest need.

Unity. The basic objective of unity was defined as creating a program that "is not merely internally coherent, but sustains connections with other parts of the curriculum." The theory-of-action perspective suggests that to produce an "internally coherent" program it would have been necessary for faculty designing the courses to share the same theory-in-use about teaching and to have reached a consensus on relevant subject matter, teaching methods, and methodology. The various committees involved in designing and implementing the program certainly had some appreciation of the need for consensus among faculty in the program, and they built into the grant a summer seminar designed to produce a shared conceptual framework. For the seminar actually to unify the courses and the program, however, it would have had to directly address existing theories-in-use about teaching and produce a new shared model. That this did not occur seems apparent from faculty reactions to the planning seminar.

- I was disappointed in the planning seminar. It was an administrative task to draft the statement of the conceptual framework, not an academic one. We should have spent more time in academic seminars on the topics and issues.
- The time given to policy was something I disapproved of. We should have given more to an exchange of ideas about courses.
- It was difficult to come to any agreement on meaning and terms in the seminar because of great differences in the background of participants. We couldn't agree on what was important.
- It was safer to draft proposals than to directly assault the subject matter.
- That summer seminar was a sheer waste of energy, trying to write paragraphs describing what we were doing.

It is clear that the faculty had some awareness that agreement with program advocates on basic approaches had not been and probably could not be reached in the seminars. Nevertheless, the seminars ran their entire course, and the group produced a written conceptual framework even though participants continued to disagree about the aims of the program and appeared to believe that they could not come to a consensus about its specific content. While faculty members saw the seminar as unproductive, at least one member of the Executive Committee evaluated the seminar very differently: "My most exciting summer experience. People who had a developed sense of themselves as disciplinarians [i.e., teachers dedicated to their discipline] had that sense become blurred. There was a willingness to blend egos and to become a collective. They were very serious and hopeful." How could this person's perception of faculty reactions be so discrepant from the faculty's self-reports? The information is not really sufficient to provide an unambiguous answer. Some possibilities, however, are that the majority of faculty had not volunteered but had been cajoled into taking part; that faculty knew the committee member in charge of the seminars was highly committed to the program and so withheld their critical comments to avoid upsetting him. Also, many of these faculty already knew at the time of the seminar that their Cultures of Europe courses would be very similar to their existing courses and did not wish to object too strongly to the work in the seminar lest they become vulnerable to concerted persuasion from program advocates. Thus the committee member running the seminar could have interpreted their lack of objections as finally "coming aboard." Faculty members' self-protective strategies amounted to gamesmanship—how to go along, not make waves, get credit for doing one's part, and not be harassed for thinking of it all as a waste of energy.

Other information is consistent with this interpretation. If the seminar never examined and changed participants' basic theories-in-use about their discipline and their teaching, then it would do little to change the content or methods of the course they eventually prepared for the program. These faculty members would teach as they always had rather than in accord with the conceptual framework produced in the seminar. Faculty self-evaluations are certainly consistent with this perspective:

- My course focused on putting cultural insights into the material. Without Cultures of Europe, I'd have done that anyway.
- In some ways my course was a projection of what I'd done before.
- Cultures of Europe hasn't affected my interests; it has just allowed me to exploit old interests, which I was unable to do before.
- The course in Cultures of Europe is not all that removed from what I was doing anyway.

Interestingly, once courses were taught, it was also obvious to administrators and Executive Committee members that this was the case:

- Many [faculty] paid no attention to the program and did the same things they'd always done.

In fact, faculty not even involved in the program saw the same thing:

- It [Cultures of Europe] won't affect faculty interests. If they have been doing something anyway, they'll join the program to do what they have been. If not, they won't join.

- Many faculty saw the program as a chance to talk about things they wanted to. . . . They did not understand the commitment required to change.

Faculty knew they were not doing what was required by the program. The Executive Committee and the administration knew it. People outside the program also knew it. Despite everyone's awareness of this lack of cooperation, Executive Committee members and administrators connected with the program believed that the failure to do what was required for the program's success could not be discussed with the faculty members involved. They saw faculty members as vulnerable and did not wish to disparage what small efforts faculty had made or hurt their feelings. Everyone concerned knew there were basic problems with introducing this new program, yet individuals' inferences about and behavioral strategies toward others produced an environment wherein faculty actions could not be discussed.

There was a consistent reaction from the majority of faculty members in the program: The program did not affect the content, perspective, or manner of instruction in the Cultures of Europe courses. (The only people who did not respond in this way were a few junior faculty, whose responses will be presented separately.) We might expect that courses based on a heterogeneous set of views of teaching would lack the internal unity and coherency advocated in the grant. Evaluations of faculty in and out of the program support this expectation.

- The courses in the program are very heterogeneous, and I can't see how they will go together to make a program. The interconnections between courses aren't clear.
- There is no apparent continuity to the program. There is not sufficient structure to identify which courses are intended for which audience . . . a program cannot exist if there is not a progression for students to see.
- The subject matter is too diverse to be considered a program. There are too many topics and no relationship between courses.

- Cultures of Europe doesn't lead to integration.
- The only way to get people to be interdisciplinary is to insist that they do so. They won't go out on their own and change their approach to subject matter.

The second component of the goal of program unity was to sustain connections with other parts of the curriculum. To do this, it would have been necessary for faculty members in existing departments to see the program as complementary to their own disciplines. Instead, they saw it as in competition, and to keep such competition from making inroads into their own enrollments and threatening their claim to resources, they quite naturally maximized the distance between the Cultures of Europe Program and their own departmental offerings. This "distancing" strategy included using as few departmental faculty in the program as possible, emphasizing the differences between departmental and Cultures of Europe offerings, and treating the program as a separate entity. Thus, although curricular connections were advocated as part of the Cultures of Europe, a team of outside evaluators assessed the program and were struck by the opposite: "The self-enclosed character of the program major creates a purely competitive relationship among departments that is both hazardous and educationally limiting." Faculty outside the program were also aware of this isolation: "They [Cultures of Europe faculty] tried to make the program exclusive. They cut off contact rather than building bridges." Whether program advocates too were aware of the nature of this competitiveness is unknown, but they certainly were heirs to its consequences. They reported that "faculty warned students away from Cultures of Europe, and when we tried to staff the program, departments couldn't spare a person."

Here is another paradox about the program. The objective was to unify Cultures of Europe with the general curriculum, but the result was an isolated, competitive program. The answer to the problem of how one can actively espouse and apparently want to achieve one objective but in practice achieve its opposite is tied up in the undiscussed conflict between program designers and faculty. The program designers created a program to meet their own objectives and then expected the faculty to enact a program that would destroy what it valued.

Redundancy and Competition. Another objective of the Cultures of Europe Program was to reduce redundancy in course content and competitiveness among faculty for student enrollment. Competition for students was, of course, based on the need to justify current levels of support and staffing. Removal of the language requirements and the subsequent loss of about one third of their enrollment had placed the language departments at a singular disadvantage. Most of these departments made few changes in their basic offerings, but they began to add courses designed to attract additional enrollment. To the extent that these new courses were successful, other departments tended to lose enrollment. As a result, several of these other departments began adding attractive courses. With a fixed number of students to divide among the various departments, competition was inevitable. Since faculty members could teach only a fixed number of courses per semester, they appeared to try out various courses to see which would attract the most students and then offer those courses at intervals that maximized enrollment.

This "solution" to the problem of protecting the status of one's discipline led to a proliferation of courses in departments already under pressure. Course preparation alone was a continual, time-consuming task. The pressures on faculty time made it reasonable to reduce the work of preparing new courses by utilizing work already done in other courses. The result was an increase in redundancy as well as competition.

Two types of course offerings emerged for language departments, one central to the study of their discipline and one intended to draw enrollment so that the study of their discipline could survive. When the Cultures of Europe Program added its courses to the curriculum, it became an additional competitor for enrollment. As a result, adding the program actually increased faculty competitiveness. It was inconsistent for Cultures of Europe supporters to advocate reducing competition and redundancy while they actually acted to increase both, and faculty members were well aware of this inconsistency:

- I don't see how it [Cultures of Europe] could reduce competition as long as it's tied to body count.

- The program will increase competitiveness on the departmental level.
- People see the program as a threat to their enrollment.
- I wish Cultures of Europe would show that two or more departments could work together. I see no instance of this.
- To the extent that you have to give up something else to do Cultures of Europe, it will increase competition.
- I never did see how the program could reduce competition.

What conditions might have reduced competition? If departments had reduced the number of their offerings and used the faculty time made available to staff Cultures of Europe courses, they could have reduced the total number of courses and thus increased enrollment in those remaining. They did not do this because to reduce competitiveness they would have had to give up staff and enrollment to Cultures of Europe, and to do that would threaten their identity as a department, potentially reduce their claim to resources and staffing, and strengthen their competitors.

Innovation and Experimentation. Innovation and experimentation, a third program objective, would have been encouraged to the extent that faculty members and departments examined and changed their theories-in-use. If theories-in-use were not changed, faculty members could behave differently—that is, they could offer new courses—but those courses would reflect the same weighting of material and the same approach to the discipline as had existed in previous courses. Innovation would require that conditions in the institution change so that faculty and administrators could explicitly examine factors which reinforced single-loop behavior and make explicit the sources of error in existing theories-in-use. As much of this analysis has tried to show, such conditions did not usually exist, and thus experimentation and innovation were difficult, risky, and rare.

Individuals within the institution knew how difficult innovation was, and many saw efforts to change as doomed from the start. Their experience led them to see the institution as rigid and inflexible, and their colleagues as reactionary and plodding. They expected things to remain the same and were apathetic because of previous failures to change. Their attitude toward the institution was reflected in comments about the ultimate impact they believed the program would have on individuals and on the curriculum.

- There is no better than an even chance for a major impact. When it is over, good, solid, able people will be the same. The turkeys will be the same.
- You can't expect old-timers to be daring.
- It's doubtful if we can speak of the program as a viable entity.
- The older [faculty] tend to regard innovation as frills or encroachment on their enrollment.
- The program will collapse.
- The program may die completely and leave rancor in its wake.
- I see the program in slow, terminal cancer.

By the end of the first two years of the grant even the once-optimistic Executive Committee members had similar views:

- I am somewhat discouraged. I had hoped for a neutral attitude [toward the change] from campus, but people outside are so negative.
- Discussions with the faculty about Cultures of Europe only stimulate self-interest.
- There are those who not only want to simplify the program, but want to do away with it all together.

Judging by the reactions of faculty members, the difficulty of getting staff, and the reluctance of college curricular review bodies to approve courses proposed for the program, the Cultures of Europe Program was a source of conflict in terms of the pragmatics of distributing resources and in terms of its violation of faculty members' governing values about curriculum, disciplinary study, and/or liberal education.

Relief to Areas of Greatest Distress. The heart of the objectives for the Cultures of Europe Program was an effort to "restore dignity to foreign language study." While stated in general terms, program designers intended to meet this objective by (1) producing a program useful to the languages in a pragmatic way, (2) relieving them of the burden of the numbers game, (3) channeling students into [language] courses once considered so essential that students were legislated into them, (4) allowing retention and strengthening of faculty in the humanities, (5) restoring curricular balance, revitalizing faculty, and providing an excellent program attractive to the entire student body. Program advocates, foreign language faculty, and those faculty members outside of the program felt that these objectives were worthwhile and important to the health of the institution. Further, these individuals were willing to cooperate and/or take an active part in a program that would achieve these objectives. How is it that these major groups could agree on the objectives of a program, yet be unable to work together to achieve them?

Program advocates and foreign language faculty each saw these abstract program objectives as consistent with their efforts on one hand to maintain their discipline, and on the other to work toward a financially sound institution. These conflicting objectives combined with Model I theories-in-use to distort both groups' interpretation of the program and translate the general objectives into very different specific actions. Language departments tried to use the Cultures of Europe Program to protect the existing language curriculum. Program advocates saw it as a way of making it easy for the languages to move away from their current programming. Language departments believed that their goals would be served if they could continue to teach primarily language courses, require extensive language as part of the program, and maintain or expand staff and resources devoted to language departments. Program advocates wanted to produce a program with a minimal language requirement or none; increase enrollment by creating an attractive, nonlanguage program; reduce the cost of maintaining the foreign languages; and institute an interdepartmental curricular planning body.

The incompatibility of these beliefs and actions was one source of continual misunderstandings, conflict, and mistrust. Model I self-sealing processes kept both groups from detecting the basic differences in interpretation. When program advocates made it clear that a language requirement was out of the question, language faculty first reacted with confusion, because they did not see how the program could meet their interpretation of the objectives without such a requirement, and then with mistrust, because the distorting effects of their theories-in-use led them to infer that the program advocates were espousing one objective and then acting in ways inconsistent with obtaining it. Since faculty saw the advocates as not acting to achieve the stated program goals, they inferred that the grant effort must have a purpose other than what they had been told. For example:

- It came from the Dean's Office. . . . They went out to get the money, not strengthen the humanities. I'm skeptical about benefits to the humanities.
- The purpose of the grant was to get money for the institution.
- There was a desire to get money. I don't see the grant as a spin-off from any of the departments.
- The proposal was to take up the gap in the languages and employ them.

Program advocates saw the proposals from the languages as unresponsive to financial and enrollment realities and they understood language resistance to the program in terms of inferred faculty resistance to change, laziness, unreasonableness, and unawareness of their own self-interests.

Since language faculty saw the program that was developed and enacted as opposed to their needs, it should not be surprising that they found little in it to give them relief:

- It has had minimal positive impact on the language departments.
- I don't see any benefits coming to the languages.
- The impact has not been great and possibly negative. Without Cultures of Europe, the languages would have done the same things.
- I don't see any impact.

The views of nonlanguage faculty were similar:

- The only impact I know of is negative. Language faculty see the program as the enemy.
- The languages resent Cultures of Europe. They're still mad that

the language requirement was dropped and their numbers sliced.

- It was supposed to have been a foreign language relief bill. It hasn't revived the foreign languages.

Overall Effects of the Program

Both faculty and program advocates felt the Cultures of Europe Program fell short of its stated goals and felt discouraged by the conflict that surrounded it. The reasons for the failure are complex and involve a number of factors, among them (1) the different interpretations of program goals by faculty and program advocates, (2) the role of Model I theories-in-use in distorting and suppressing information, (3) interpersonal processes which made basic issues undiscussable, and (4) self-sealing processes that kept critical issues and information undiscovered.

Few individuals in the institution were surprised at the program's lack of acceptance and success. Many had predicted just such a result from their own experiences within the institution. These predictions are important because they emphasize faculty members' and administrators' shared perception of the institution's inability to meet the problems confronting it. The results of the Cultures of Europe experience characterize a basic issue facing the institution: To survive and prosper the institution, the faculty, and administrators within it must be able to produce effective solutions to financial, curricular, and personnel problems, but the institution's behavioral world acts to decrease the probability of finding and enacting those solutions. The institution needed to change its own behavioral world before it could effectively address the problems that motivated the original development effort.

Junior Faculty: A Different Experience

The junior faculty associated with the Cultures of Europe Program warrant separate consideration because their reactions to the program were qualitatively different from the faculty considered thus far. Although this group is small, its responses are important for illustrating some of the conditions that produce significant change in individuals and elicit enthusiasm and commitment.

Commitment. The program had a very large effect on how junior faculty viewed and taught their subject matter. While senior faculty indicated that Cultures of Europe had produced little change in their approach to their disciplines, junior faculty reacted very differently. For example:

- Personally, I am very absorbed in the program. I'm reading cultural history and find it hard to go back to my old way of analysis. I find the whole experience very invigorating.
- It has changed my thinking in my own area. It has allowed some doubts to come out. It is an opportunity to create a course and an approach.

While the new approach offered by the program was time-consuming and ultimately increased their workload, junior faculty accepted the extra work at the same time that they remained aware of the risk to their careers:

- I knew it would be a risk since I'm an untenured faculty member. I thought it was worth it for personal development.
- I decided I could make a contribution even though I was concerned about spreading myself too thin by trying to keep active in two or three areas.

Because junior faculty were initially excited by the intellectual challenge of a new methodology, they willingly devoted time and energy both to their own professional development and to the construction of a quality program. They saw themselves as having much to offer, were somewhat intolerant of less involved faculty, and resented faculty members who did not do what, in their view, was required by the program.

- There is a complaint about the program I think should be expressed for myself and other faculty. Cultures of Europe offers $2000 to junior faculty. Out of that they want a great course and a publication. Senior faculty are paid $2000 to repackage old stuff. The senior faculty aren't doing much in the program, with some notable exceptions. I think we should bag the notion of revitalizing senior faculty.

- I am biased in saying that the junior faculty are very, very committed to the program and enthusiastic about it. I can't make that blanket statement about senior faculty.
- The most important impact of this program would be to get the senior faculty to do *something*.

Acceptance of Goals. One of the striking differences between junior and senior faculty members was their perception of the goals of the program. The senior faculty typically perceived the goals of the program in negative terms:

- They went out to get the money, not strengthen the humanities.
- The program was intended to give Professors X and Y something to do.
- It was designed to save the languages and get money.
- The financial impetus, the original groundswell came from the dean, not the faculty.
- The purpose was to get money for the institution.

In contrast, junior faculty perceived the goals in academic and programmatic terms. They saw the program as intended "to allow students to perceive knowledge as less fragmented and to provide a new role for the humanities"; "to revitalize the humanities"; "to find a new focus for the humanities"; and "to give identity to creation of a solid program in the humanities."

It was this difference in perceived goals that enabled the junior faculty to accept and commit themselves to the program and to be willing to experiment. Theoretically, their willingness to adopt a different approach to their own discipline lies in their theories-in-use about teaching and curriculum. Theories-in-use about the conduct of a discipline gradually develop out of conscious decisions about the goals and strategies of teaching. Over time, they are learned so well that they are tacitly held and applied. The junior faculty, at an early point in their careers, were explicitly concerned about developing an intellectual definition of their discipline and their own professional lives. While such definitions normally come from their own departments, it may have been the case that Cultures of Europe offered both a place to define and examine their approach as well as sufficient support to encourage such activities before departmental goals were internalized. When coupled with the inherent attraction of an interdisciplinary approach, the existence of an alternative and support to pursue it could have allowed junior faculty to incorporate the interdisciplinary approach of Cultures of Europe into their own theories-in-use. Indeed, even after the grant period, junior faculty still found the program intellectually satisfying, exciting, and challenging:

- I've been affected. I'm using some of the process analysis in my seminar now. I feel I have done more and am more insightful.
- Cultures of Europe is a small part of my teaching, but accounts for most of my writing.
- Part of the material I teach in my other classes is boring for students. This approach gets them interested in what wouldn't have fascinated them before.
- It's been good for me. A chance to try something new. A chance to go outside a narrow discipline. My courses now come from Cultures of Europe. I also got an article from this work.

It appears that the interdisciplinary approach has become permanently incorporated into these individuals' professional activities.

Learning the Institutional Theory-in-Use. At the same time that these new faculty members learned an approach to their discipline, they also learned how to get along within the institution. Since new faculty are not usually aware of the details of the institutional functioning, they were initially unaware of conflicts between departments, administration, and individual faculty. They had yet to learn that those who espoused the same academic goals might not agree on the means by which to meet them.

At the beginning of the grant period, junior faculty saw few reasons why the objectives of the program could not be met. Indeed, they fully expected to meet or at least come close to meeting all the program goals. By the end of the grant period, however, their optimism had greatly changed. While they had benefited from the program intellectually, they had also learned a great deal about the behavioral world that any effort to produce change had to face. Many of their comments at the end of the grant were directed by their increased awareness of the institution's behavioral world.

- On the whole, the college is resistant to change.
- While I'm enthusiastic about the program, I don't doubt that it will fall on hard times, die a slow death.
- Political things have destroyed an opportunity.
- There has been strong resistance from departments.
- To teach in the Cultures of Europe you have to cut one course from your department, and some feel we should support our departments at all costs.

These comments are significant and point to an important consequence of the junior faculty members' experience with the Cultures of Europe Program. As the program progressed, they quickly learned a great deal about the institutional theory-in-use. They learned that change was difficult, that innovation was opposed because it threatened existing departments, that departmental interests could hold out against efforts to change, and that departmental loyalty was an important means for obtaining one's goals or just surviving. They also learned something that they will apply every time a new attempt to innovate is made: that is, they will know that results are seldom worth the tremendous energy, politicking, and persuasion necessary to produce them. With these insights, the probability that these faculty will be interested in working for any change in the future is decreased.

New faculty's decreased willingness to participate reinforces the rigidity of Liberal College. Yet for the institution to solve problems it is necessary that individuals be willing to work for change. The result is a paradox in which the institution must change to survive but attempts to introduce changes increase resistance to change. The resulting behavioral world then becomes a source of increasing organizational entropy fed and sustained by individuals' Model I theories-in-use.

5

❖❖❖❖❖❖❖❖❖

Increasing
Effectiveness
by Changing
Theories-in-Use

❖❖❖❖❖❖❖❖❖❖❖❖❖❖❖❖❖❖❖

This book began with a general
discussion of some of the difficult problems facing institutions of
higher education: internal and external pressures caused by decreasing enrollment, decreasing funds, expanding academic fields, and
the growing need to redistribute resources among departments. Liberal College was examined as an example of a high-quality institution trying to respond to these pressures by changing its curriculum,
faculty, and organizational structure. The effort began in an atmos-
phere of optimism, because the need for change was obvious to most
faculty members and administrators, who seemed willing to alter the
institution and their personal careers significantly. Nevertheless,
efforts to design and carry out the Cultures of Europe program
provoked so much resistance that even after three years few changes
had occurred, and the program itself was characterized by errors and
conflict.

In Chapter Four I suggested that the sources of the conflict and errors were rooted in individuals' theories-in-use. Because faculty members and administrators had only a Model I theory-in-use for designing their actions, all their efforts to solve problems involved attempts to unilaterally control others. Because theories-in-use function tacitly, these individuals remained unaware of the deeper meanings and unintended consequences of their actions and were unable to design actions not aimed at controlling others. Consequently, they never effectively addressed the reasons for resistance to change. Important issues became undiscussable, and opposition to the program spread widely through the humanities departments, while resistance went underground. Ultimately the program failed to attract sufficient faculty or student interest and achieved few—if any—of its original objectives.

Model I concepts help to explain some of the dynamics behind the change attempt at Liberal College, but such insights go only halfway toward breaking the single-loop cycle. They located the source of the problem, but accurate diagnosis is not sufficient to produce effective change. A theory-of-action analysis implies that the only effective way to deal with problems like those that plagued Liberal College is to change individuals' theories-in-use. The rest of this chapter examines the process of learning a new theory-in-use and the problems that people encounter as they attempt to do so. Since the theory-of-action approach has been used more frequently to diagnose individual and organizational problems than to change underlying theories-in-use, the methods for teaching are not as well developed as the diagnostic procedures; however, we know enough to gain useful insights from an examination of the processes involved in learning a new theory-in-use.

Basic Components of Learning Model II

As Argyris and Schön pointed out in the passage quoted in Chapter Three, learning Model II behavioral strategies does not mean learning to do the opposite of Model I. The opposite of Model I would be "not trying to maximize winning" or "not trying to achieve one's goals." A person using such strategies turns control over to others and refuses to actively deal with issues. Model II strategies are proactive. A person using Model II takes and strongly advocates a position in a way that encourages others to confront the weaknesses and consequences of the position and to inquire into the reasoning behind it. Model II behavioral strategies encourage people to jointly test the validity of inferences, evaluations, and attributed motives. The use of Model II strategies maximizes information available for solving problems and making decisions. Learning Model II does not mean abandoning the use of Model I—that is neither possible nor desirable. Rather, one gradually learns a new theory-of-action and recognizes the right moment to use it.

The role of emotions. Most people find two things about the theory-of-action approach very disturbing. First, they are upset when they see how much of their own behavior consists of Model I strategies. Second, they are distressed to find that they cannot change their actions by a simple effort of will. Their response—a combination of anger and frustration—is both a major obstacle and an important opportunity for learning a different model for action. Occasionally emotional reactions are so strong that people temporarily stop trying to change their actions and lose the ability to critically examine them. Effective learning occurs when people accept being sidetracked by anger over their failures and then use the anger as a guide to the source of their failures. Later parts of this chapter deal with emotionality in more detail, but it should be emphasized here that learning Model II is not only an intellectual task. It is a difficult experience that generates considerable discomfort, anxiety, and self-doubt. The cycle of emotional response, successful action, and new frustration is a major feature of learning a new theory-of-action.

The skill of the instructor. The instructor's ability to demonstrate Model II skills consistently is critical for the success of a seminar designed to teach those skills. People readily infer the principles underlying the instructor's actions from his behavior. If these actions do not reflect Model II governing values, those being taught will easily detect the inconsistency. The instructor must explicitly state and strongly advocate his position while encouraging others to test its usefulness. He must teach them how to compare his behavior with their own so that they can judge the usefulness of the theory-of-action approach for themselves.

The use of heuristics. Interrupting behavior patterns that occur automatically and bridging the gap between insight and action are two of the hardest tasks in learning Model II. Heuristics are designed to help people substitute new, more effective actions for old patterns of behavior.

A heuristic is a mini-program that can be used to replace a segment of a current behavior pattern. It is a brief, easily remembered tool for acting more effectively. A heuristic has three components: a *"flag"* or clear specification of when it should be used; a *recognition* of what is going on in the situation at a correct level; and a concise, usable prescription for what to *say* or how to *act* to another person. If possible, an allusion to the theory underlying the prescribed action should be made. The specification of when the heuristic should be used serves as a cognitive reminder flag to help people recognize that they should interrupt their behavior and try to change the theory-in-use producing it. In some senses, a good heuristic represents a piece of the theory-in-use to be learned.

The heuristics included in this chapter are designed to help decrease dependence on an instructor. The theory-of-action approach and the heuristics themselves seek not only to teach the skills needed to solve the users' own problems, but also to enable them to teach similar skills to others.

Heuristics presented in the early stages of learning are designed to help users test the applicability of the theory-of-action to their own behavior. Subsequent heuristics help them break automatic Model I action patterns and enact Model II strategies. Heuristics enable production of short segments of Model II behavior so that users can form their own judgments about the effectiveness of the alternative theory-of-action. In the last stage of learning, users learn to design their own heuristics for situations specific to their institutions. They also return to heuristics the instructor used at the beginning of the seminar and use them to teach the skills they have learned to their colleagues.

A good heuristic is very powerful, because with its aid a person can learn to recognize counterproductive behavior, then follow through to effective action. The heuristic specifies the connection between recognition and action and provides a behavioral prescription for what to do. This makes it easier for a beginner to enact a segment of Model II behavior and test its effectiveness.

Stages of Learning Model II

The skills and methods for teaching Model II are not nearly so well developed as procedures for using Model I to diagnose errors in individual and organizational action. However, we know enough to identify some of the stages of learning Model II and to specify what individuals must learn at one stage before they can progress to the next.

This chapter uses examples from a seminar designed to teach Model II skills. The seminar met periodically for approximately ten days during the year. The examples illustrate problems and objectives unique to each of the learning stages and convey the participants' reactions to their own and others' attempts to learn a new theory-in-use. The teaching methods used in the seminar address the difficulty of making tacit processes explicit, demonstrate the use of heuristics to interrupt the automatic functioning of current theories-in-use, focus on bridging the action gap, and emphasize the role of the instructor in facilitating learning and increasing the independence of seminar participants. In general, participants depend heavily on the expertise of the instructor in the early stages of learning. As the seminar progresses, they become better able to direct their own learning and to deal more with institutional problems. By the end of the seminar, participants are largely independent of the instructor.

Stage One: Testing the Model

Participants typically begin with a question: "This theory seems very interesting, but does it have anything to do with our institution?" The seminar recounted in this chapter began when several university administrators, including the president, expressed enough interest to pursue this question. They arranged to meet with the instructor periodically in a seminar format to see if the approach could help them understand some of the problems their institution faced. They committed themselves only to finding out whether Model I gave them new insights into institutional problems. Both the participants and the instructor planned to evaluate the usefulness of the approach at the end of the seminar. If Model I seemed to fit the institution's problems, then the administrators would decide whether learning Model II was worth the effort. The limited-objective format minimized participants' commitment, gave them an opportunity to learn what the approach had to offer, and maximized their freedom to choose whether to continue.

Because theoretical concepts are best learned in the context of actual behavior, the administrators brought examples from their own experience to use in the seminar. The examples were presented in the case study format used in Chapter Three. These brief scenarios about important incidents in the participants' experience provided information about individuals' theories-in-use and about the general environment of their institutions. The case material allowed participants to bring their real problems into the seminar and to use them to learn about the theory-of-action approach. Some of them selected situations in which they felt they had been particularly effective, while others presented instances of what they felt were ineffective actions. Both types of cases reflected the underlying Model I theory-in-use and its characteristic unintended consequences.

Before participants could even consider trying a change program based on the theory-of-action, they had to learn of the existence, strength, and pervasiveness of their own tacit processes. They had to discover the Model I meanings in their own actions and try to change them before they could know how difficult and upsetting it is to try to interrupt behavior that occurs automatically. Only then would they have enough information and experience to evaluate the approach and decide whether to learn an alternative theory-of-action.

Relevance of theory-of-action for participants. The first seminar objective was to have participants test the applicability of Model I to their own actions as presented in their individual cases. This was possible because, while individuals seldom see their own actions as unilaterally controlling, inconsistent, or counterproductive, others are often well aware of these strategies.

People interested in increasing their effectiveness are usually unaware of any discrepancy between their espoused theories-of-action and their theories-in-use. They believe that they can accurately verbalize the rules that govern their actions, and they are unaware of the unintended consequences of those actions. The effort required to cope with the rush of immediate events typically overwhelms any inclination to examine internal processes. As a result, inferences are often mistaken for facts and actions are designed to fit an erroneous picture of reality. There is an inclination to worry more about what to say next than about the consequences of what has already been said.

Seminar participants were good at pointing out the discrepancy between the effects that a colleague intended to produce in his sample case and the actual effects of the behavior described. One of the problems immediately encountered in these discussions was that the interactions described in the cases were filled with unacknowledged inferences, attributed motives, and evaluations. Seminar participants found it difficult to connect abstractions to specific events in a colleague's case. For example, consider the following condensation of one case used in the seminar. The situation involved a dean who had been in charge of a major school in the university for three years. During that time the school had consistently run in the red and had encountered numerous other problems. The president had talked to the dean about these problems over a period of months prior to the conversation described here.

The president wrote the following dialogue. His goal in the interaction was to "have an open discussion with the person about his deanship and his potential to develop."

Underlying thoughts	*Dialogue*
We're dealing with a good man's career. Lay it out straight. Don't prejudge him though I certainly lean toward a change in deans. Keep my mind open.	*President:* Dean, I don't believe that the school is being built up. Key administrators have resigned; morale is low; some chairpersons have had to be removed. While some good things have happened, on the whole, things just aren't clicking. I don't see a good, positive spirit in the school.
	I'd like to discuss the best resolution. There seem to be three choices: another deanship elsewhere in the university, leave the university, or

Underlying thoughts

Dialogue

do what is necessary here. I don't know the right answer. I'd like to arrive at the best choice.

If he doesn't have to worry about his income for a reasonable time and I don't have to worry about the problems of a lame duck, perhaps we can be more fully open for this discussion.

I'd like to talk to you free from the pressures of protecting interests. In other words, I'd like to avoid the problems attendant with lame duck deans and also relieve you of a gap in your income.

Dean: What do you think are the reasons for these conditions and results? What is it I do or don't do?

I'd like to help him, but I don't know the answer.

President: I believe the problem rests in your leadership. There's a lack of spirit in the school. Complaints come to me rather than to you. There's a high turnover of key personnel. You seem to lack a sense of proprietorship. What causes this? I don't know.

Dean. What do you think? I'm not trying to put you on the spot, but I have a lot of respect for you.

After some additional discussion the dean was asked to take a month to think things over and then to get together with the president again to "see where things stood." As a consequence of this discussion, the dean decided to resign from the university and seek a new job.

In analyzing the case, participants spotted an inconsistency between the president's words and his intentions. First, while he himself believed that he had an open mind and was willing to consider all possible alternatives, the participants inferred (as had the dean) from the president's comments about "lame-duck deans" and "protecting income" that he had already decided to let the dean go. As a result the important fact—being fired—was undiscussable. Second, the president did nothing to help the dean learn from his experience so that he might be more effective in this or a subsequent job. Although the president was unaware of these aspects of his actions at the time he wrote the case, he agreed that this analysis seemed reasonable. He was both surprised and upset that he had not realized the effect he was having at the time of the conversation.

In summarizing his initial reaction to the conversation, the president had said: "I thought I was making it clear in a friendly way that he had not done what was expected and that he had to come around to keep his job." Two other participants saw the interaction differently. Their evaluations illustrate the strength of their reactions and their own use of abstractions.

- Boy, that sure was Model I. You really reared back and clobbered him.
- What I see is that you didn't put yourself in the other fellow's position. Understand what's in his mind, then let him know what's in yours.

Neither of these remarks were tied to specific parts of the president's dialogue with the dean. Seminar participants were generally unaware that their discussions were so abstract. From the theory-of-action perspective, one must become aware of using abstractions and learn to connect them to directly observable actions in order to identify the source of a problem and decide how to solve it. The instructor presented a heuristic to help participants become aware of the problem.

Making Participants Aware of Their Use of Abstractions

Flag: When participants discuss important events at an abstract level,

Recognize that abstract, unillustrated discussions are not tied to any specific behaviors and thus preclude effective action.

Say: I see this discussion as very abstract. While it may be very interesting, it is hard to move from these abstractions to recommendations that would help the president improve his effectiveness. To avoid this, I'd suggest that we move the discussion to the specifics of his actual behavior.

or

You've said he "really reared back and clobbered him." I see this as an inference. That interpretation may be perfectly correct. My problem is that because it is abstract, it could mean

one thing to you and another to me. I believe it's important to
avoid the possibility of any misunderstanding. Can you tell me
what he did or said that led you to your inference?

Both these interventions are designed to make individuals
aware that their current conceptualization of a problem is only indirectly tied to observable events. They probably do not know exactly
what behavior caused the problem, so they cannot identify the
behavior that should change to increase the person's effectiveness.
This heuristic also contained instructions for beginning a levels-of-
meaning analysis. Illustrating inferences with specifics is easily con-
verted into inferring the social meanings inherent in actions.

As participants begin focusing on directly observable behavior, they also begin learning to test in public alternative interpretations of a situation in ways that minimize win-lose dynamics and
maximize the availability of valid information. "In a friendly way"
and "clobbered him" are examples of alternative interpretations of
the same incident. Disputants typically resolve such disagreements
by trying to persuade each other that one view is the correct one.
Persuasion is an attempt to justify one abstraction with another.
Since another abstraction doesn't help, disagreements are usually
settled by means of status and power rather than valid information.
Learning Model II requires that one become aware of the tendency
to use abstractions and then learn how to avoid the negative consequences of abstract disagreements and discussions.

Dealing with the Consequences of Abstract Arguments

Flag: When participants argue for a position at an abstract level,

Recognize that continuing at an abstract level establishes
win-lose dynamics, further commits each person to one position, and increases the need for saving face.

Say: To resolve your disagreement, I would like to
recommend that we test these interpretations by going to the
data. What else do you see in the case that is either consistent or
inconsistent with your positions?

In the case of the president and the dean, focusing attention
on the data separated the task of finding specific actions relevant to

both sides of the disagreement from counterproductive, ego-involving argument. This heuristic changed the focus from "Who is going to win?" to "Which interpretation is most consistent with the available information?" This change was especially important because the president was frustrated when he discovered that others viewed as destructive the actions he had felt were particularly effective. If the emotion generated by a win-lose argument had been added to that frustration, he probably would have invested more effort in winning the argument than in learning to act more effectively.

Seminar participants sometimes engaged in long discussions and arguments because they did not have sufficient information in the written case material to resolve conflicting interpretations. To disrupt the win-lose dynamics, it was important to direct their energy toward generation of new information. The following heuristic was designed for that purpose:

Dealing with Unresolvable Conflict

Flag: When win-lose arguments develop,

Recognize that participants need some alternative method for resolving disagreements and that specifying the information that would settle the issue is one such method.

Say: I do not see how we can settle this disagreement with the information available. If you agree that we cannot solve the problem without more information, what kind of information could we gather that you would accept as disconfirming your interpretations? What could we do to get that information?

This intervention changed the focus of interactions from argument to hypothesis-testing and produced explicit statements of what information would lead each participant involved in the argument to see his own position differently. Each of them helped to specify rationally the critical test, so that when the information was produced they could view changes in their own positions as reasonable and logical. Hypothesis-testing makes people less likely to experience changes in their positions as defeats and it gives them direct experience with techniques for producing information that would otherwise be unavailable.

Occasionally anger or blindness to the possibility of error led a seminar participant to reply to the request for hypothesis-testing with "There is nothing that would lead me to change my mind." People use such statements to insulate themselves from information and to unilaterally end discussions. While they certainly have the right to do so, it is useful to determine if they are aware of what they are doing.

Creating Awareness of Defensiveness

Flag: If someone avows his determination to ignore information,

Recognize that the person has made a statement about his unwillingness to learn and that he may not be aware of it. His emotional reaction may be affecting his judgment.

Say: That presents a serious problem for me. It does seem that we can clarify this issue by getting more information about the situation or about people's reaction to it. I hear you saying that you will ignore whatever information we may develop. If that is true, then I must conclude that you are more interested in defending your own position than in testing it. What is your reaction to my inferences?

The instructor used this heuristic to help the participant evaluate his own distortions of information and openness to learning. It makes one of the negative consequences of the Model I governing value—"minimizing losing"—very salient: the person resolutely fighting for his or her position often appears irrational and defensive.

Participants learned from these discussions and from the use of these heuristics that Model I did seem to apply to the actions they had recorded in their cases. As the seminar continued in this stage of learning, the instructor presented Model I in more detail, illustrated levels-of-meaning analysis, and used actions from the cases and from interactions in the seminar to illustrate as many of the theoretical processes as possible. In general the instructor attempted to demonstrate how to produce valid information and maximize free choice.

Robustness of Model I actions. Participants' doubts and reservations about the usefulness of the theory-of-action approach did not disappear when they found that Model I fit their actions.

Instead, they asserted one of two things: some insisted that although their actions were consistent with Model I in *that* case, they now understood and could produce Model II behavior; others saw that their actions reflected Model I governing values, but maintained that Model I was the only way to be effective in the real world. Both positions indicated that participants had learned a great deal about the use of Model I for understanding the dynamics of their previous actions. They had not learned how hard it is to produce actions that are inconsistent with individuals' current theories-in-use. Since Model I governing values operate automatically, all their actions have Model I meanings, even when they try to alter them. At this stage of learning, the focus was on helping participants recognize how difficult it is to change tacitly produced action patterns. This experience is important because people are unwilling to try to change a tacit theory until they discover how robust an effect it has on their actions and how negative some of the consequences of those actions are. Once more, a heuristic aids the necessary learning.

Experiencing the Robustness of One's Theory-in-Use

Flag: When participants assert that they now understand and can produce Model II behavior,

Recognize that they have learned to identify aspects of Model I behavioral strategies in their actions, but that they have not experienced the difficulty of producing actions inconsistent with their existing theory-in-use.

Say: You may be right However, my experience and the theory suggest it will be very hard for you to do so. But we can test this possibility. For example, one thing we can do is to have you take the role of the president in our current case. What would you say in his place that would be more effective in addressing the problems you have identified in the interaction?

Each participant in the seminar then tried to produce actions that embodied Model II rather than Model I meanings. Other members of the seminar subjected each attempt to a levels-of-meaning analysis and found that even when a participant produced action that he felt was effective, the others still saw it as unilaterally controlling, ineffective, and consistent with Model I. The person who had attempted to produce the alternative meanings frequently reacted with bewilderment and frustration to his inability to break his Model I action patterns. His colleagues continued to find Model I meanings in his actions, even when he was given numerous opportunities to design responses reflecting Model II meanings. These repeated failures greatly increased participants' frustration as well as their awareness of the robustness of their current theories-in-use. For some, the changes in awareness were dramatic:

- What impresses me is that although these cases aren't long, we've tried for an hour to do better and none of us have.
- I'm surprised at the clarity of Model I behavior. I have a lot more to learn about Model II.
- I've intellectualized all the assumptions of Model II, but something keeps me from acting it.
- I still see myself as Model I. When I try to create Model II behavior, I feel as if I'm trying to write with my feet.

These experiences were important for the administrators in the seminar because it provided the information and personal experience necessary for evaluating the usefulness of the theory-in-action approach. Awareness of the robustness of their Model I behavior signaled that they could now detect the deeper levels of meaning that distinguish Model II from Model I. However, because of their frustration with the robustness of their Model I theories-in-use, participants' objections to the theory-of-action approach took on a completely different character. Instead of asserting that Model II actions were easy for them to produce, they now maintained, in effect, that if they couldn't produce Model II meanings, it was impossible for anyone to do so. They felt that they had learned enough about the theory to find Model I meanings in virtually any action. In order to progress to the next stage, they had to become able to distinguish the characteristics of Model II action.

Demonstrating the Possibility of an Alternative Theory-in-Use

Flag: When participants are repeatedly unable to design effective actions,
Recognize that they may believe Model II actions are

impossible to achieve and that this belief creates frustration. Frustration can be useful if it motivates further learning. Participants now need to observe a Model II intervention to see what it is like and how it produces different second-level meanings and consequences.

   Act by demonstrating a Model II intervention. Then have participants analyze it as they have other interactions.

For example, the following interaction occurred in the seminar when the instructor took the role of the president in a reenactment of the previous case.

A Model II Intervention Dialogue

Dean: (from the earlier example) What do you think are the reasons for these conditions and results? What is it I do or don't do?

Instructor (as President): Dean, the question that you ask illustrates one of the problems that I have. You ask me to take initiatives and responsibility for you.

Participant: What if the dean replied, "Well, I'll take that to heart." What would you say?

Instructor (as President): I'm glad you see what I've said as helpful, but that doesn't make me feel secure or any more certain, because of your past performance. There is an enormous gap between your seeing something and your doing something about it.

Participant: Ok. That struck me. The second I heard that, I said: Why in hell didn't I think of that? It struck me as right on the mark because the response implied the diagnosis of the problem. It tells him, "All your behavior is an example of what you're doing." But how did you know to say that?

This last question provided the opportunity for the instructor to show how he had assigned a different meaning to the dean's original question and how that assigned meaning had led to his response. Participants had viewed the dean's question as a request for help. Given that inference (assigned meaning), they acted to provide the help and tried to do for the dean what he should have been doing for himself. Their efforts were ineffective, partly because their prescriptions for action were so abstract that they could not easily translate them into action (for example, "have a sense of proprietorship"; "get down to the level of the troops"), and partly because their response to the dean's request for help colluded in making him dependent on others and perpetuated his real problem.

The instructor inferred a different second-level meaning. He saw the dean as saying, "I don't understand myself. I would like you to take the responsibility for understanding me. I promise to listen and be dependent on you." Given this meaning, it was easier to see that his problem was one of dependence and lack of initiative. The intervention strategy that then made sense was to make explicit for the dean the nature of his problem. The difference in how the instructor and the participants determined the meaning of the dean's question is critical. It is related to the effect that one's governing values have on distorting information and guiding one's interpretations. Seminar participants viewed the dean's actions in the context of wanting to minimize his negative feelings and with an eye toward what they could control in the situation to produce the results they wanted. Their inferences about second-level meanings were filtered through these values, and their actions were designed on the basis of Model I objectives.

Though the process is difficult, participants can learn to avoid creating Model I meanings. They can tentatively assign meanings to events, plan actions based on those meanings, then extrapolate what the consequences might be. If the results are undesirable, they should go back and search for meanings they might have missed. For example, once participants saw that a consequence of providing help to the dean was to make him dependent on them, it became clear that dependence was the root problem. The assigned meaning of a request for help had ignored that problem. Working backwards from the consequences gave the participants a method for discovering inherent meanings they had previously missed.

Participants also learned from the instructor's demonstration that it is possible to construct actions that embody Model II meanings. The demonstration of Model II action encouraged participants to tolerate the frustration generated by their own ineffective efforts and to continue an uncomfortable learning experience.

At this point participants had experiential referents for concepts like self-sealing, theory-in-use, espoused theories, and levels-of-meaning analysis. They had learned to use the theory to analyze others' behavior and had begun to make explicit the basis for their own actions. They had seen the pervasiveness and consequences of untested abstractions, experienced the robustness of Model I behavior patterns, and compared the consequences of Model II actions with those of their own behavior. Once people reach this stage of learning, they have sufficient information to end the diagnostic phase of the seminar, determine whether the approach seems useful for their particular problems, and decide whether they wish to continue and attempt to learn how to enact Model II behaviors. In this case participants decided that they wished to continue the seminar and learn an alternative theory-in-use. In so doing, they entered the next stage of learning. This stage focuses on translating previously gained insights into new action patterns.

Stage Two: Assigning Meaning, Planning, and Enacting in Slow-Time

In the second stage of learning, participants begin to learn how to systematically enact small segments of Model II behaviors. To do so successfully, they must proceed through the steps of assigning meaning, planning an action based on that meaning, and enacting what they plan very slowly, so that they can consciously disrupt their current theories-in-use. At the stage we have been reviewing, the instructor provided simple heuristics and techniques for participants to use as aids in breaking old patterns and learning Model II patterns. Because of the interference from their existing theories-in-use, participants found it helpful to learn and practice at a very slow pace. In their first efforts they actually wrote down assigned meanings and proposals for alternative action. This technique allowed members of the group to examine the separate components of the learning process and get feedback about them. After a period of practice and increasing proficiency in this slowed-down form, participants gradually speeded up the pace of assigning meanings and designing actions.

Using this slowed-down technique participants once again had to turn their attention to the frequent use of unillustrated abstractions. They were already very skilled at spotting such abstractions, but they did not know what to do once they had detected them. The following heuristic gave them a small segment of Model II action that they could use to specify what to do to bridge that particular action gap.

Connecting Abstractions to Directly Observable Data

Flag: When you hear others make unillustrated inferences, attributions, or evaluations,

Recognize that they may create errors because of different possible interpretations. Attend to and test these abstractions before attempting to deal with anything else.

Say: What is it that you heard or saw that led you to (the abstraction)?

This heuristic helped participants produce illustrations of the abstractions they encountered. They experienced an increased sense of efficacy as they discovered information that they otherwise might have missed, and avoided misinterpreting what others said. This reduced the frustration they had been feeling.

Most of the initial attempts to enact Model II behavior patterns were lengthy and confused. Because the skills of assigning meanings and planning actions were not tacit, seminar participants often included too much in their Model II attempts. These early efforts created two problems—their actions often confused rather than helped others, and participants could not design actions that were of an appropriate length for a normal interaction. The tendency to try to deal at once with all their new insights paralyzed their ability to speak succinctly and effectively. They needed some heuristic to help them overcome that paralysis.

Overcoming Initial Barriers to Change

> *Flag:* When you find you have designed sequences of
> action that are too long, or you are paralyzed by indecision
> about where to begin,
> *Recognize* that you are inhibited by trying to address too
> many aspects of a complex situation. You can only deal with
> one aspect at a time.
> *Act* without trying to be perfect or complete.

This heuristic encouraged participants to experiment with new
action patterns. At this stage of learning it was important for them
to practice and overcome the anxiety that prevented further experimentation, even though the actions they produced might be incom-
plete. Without the expectation of perfection, they were able to
produce some approximations of Model II action that others could
identify and encourage. Participants continued to examine the
meanings inherent in their new actions. When they contained components of Model II, participants elaborated them. When actions
contained Model I meanings and consequences, participants rede-
signed them and acted again.

The slow-time learning stage was relatively short. As participants gained skill they soon wanted to speed things up to more
closely approximate live interactions. As they moved from single
actions to more complex, faster-paced interactions, this stage was
gradually transformed into the real-time interaction stage.

Stage Three: Assigning Meaning, Planning, and Enacting in Real-Time

In this learning stage, participants began to deal with the
complex behaviors and problems that they encountered at their own
institutions. They also began to focus more closely on problems that
pertained to certain individuals in the group, as well as with general
concerns that applied to most of the members. One of the latter was
the emotion generated in others and in oneself when attempting to
enact Model II. Another was the need for heuristics to flag and
interrupt some rather subtle Model I strategies that individuals continued to use. Despite these obstacles, this stage was characterized by

the growing competence of participants, decreased dependence on the instructor, and the desire to practice and master new skills.

One of the subtle intrusions of Model I encountered by participants as they tried to develop and practice new skills was a result of their belief that Model II is primarily intended to elicit information. Many participants focused their efforts on producing Model II behavior by asking questions, because they saw that as one good way to get information. For example, one of the participants, Ann, felt that she could be effective in the case used earlier. She role-played an interaction that she would have with the university president, while another participant took the role of the president.

> *Ann:* What did you infer about the dean?
> *President:* He was a good man and trying hard.
> *Ann:* Was he succeeding?
> *President:* No, not at all.
> *Ann:* What kept him from succeeding?

Participants analyzed this series of questions and concluded that Ann had already arrived at some conclusions about what the president thought and had asked questions to get confirmation of that analysis. She used questions as a device to keep her own analysis private and less subject to scrutiny or criticism. Questioning designed to lead another is a method of unilateral control—a Model I governing value. Participants needed a heuristic to help them recognize when they were engaging in such "lawyering" and learn to avoid it.

Avoiding "Lawyering"

> *Flag:* If you find yourself rehearsing a series of questions and planning additional questions on the basis of anticipated responses,
> *Recognize* that you are planning to control others by leading them to a conclusion you have already reached.
> *Act* by stating the conclusion and the data you used to get there. Then ask, "What are your views on this?"

Use of this heuristic helped participants to openly advocate their position while inquiring into alternative viewpoints. When they found that another's views were different, they had to explore the other person's perspective so that they did not cut themselves off from potentially important information. If Ann had used this heuristic instead of her series of questions, she might have said to the president, "Your talk about lame-duck deans and protecting the dean from a salary gap makes me think that you have already decided to fire him. What is your reaction to my inference?"

Participants had already learned to detect others' inferences during the slowed-down stage, but as things speeded up, they fell back into making their own untested inferences and evaluations and acting on them. They were experiencing a more complex example of the robustness of their Model I action patterns. Nevertheless, they found it hard to listen to others without making and acting on inferences. Participants sought a heuristic to help test inferences and thus maximize available information.

Ensuring that Your Evaluations Do Not Obscure Information

> *Flag:* If you find yourself thinking such things as, "This person is off on some tangent" or "That is irrelevant and silly,"
> *Recognize* that these are both evaluations. The other person may feel he is providing important information that you are missing. Part of your reaction may reflect your own inability to see the value of that information.
> *Say:* I'm having difficulty seeing how (what other said) is relevant to the point under discussion. Can you help me see the relevance?

This heuristic helped participants discover how others reasoned about a point, and it often produced important information. However, participants found it difficult to use when their inferences or evaluations about others were negative. Anticipation of others' negative reactions inhibited effectiveness, because the Model II behavior conflicted with participants' Model I governing value of minimizing negative feelings in oneself and others. This was especially true when evaluating others' performances. The conflict between the two models for action created hesitancy and anxiety. Participants needed a heuristic to correctly identify the source of the anxiety they were experiencing and to break its inhibitory effect on action.

Substituting Valid Information for Minimizing Negative Feelings

> *Flag:* When you feel anxious or concerned about how an individual is likely to react to your Model II action,
> *Recognize* that these fears represent protective strategies for minimizing your own and others' negative feelings. If you respond to these fears, you will decrease the effectiveness of your action and prevent others from gaining valid information that they might find important and useful.
> *Act:* Go ahead and enact the Model II behavior you had planned. You may be wrong about others' reactions. They may not be as vulnerable or brittle as you have inferred.

or

> If you are certain that what you say will produce negative feelings that will be counterproductive, acknowledge that possibility but state your reasons for proceeding.
> *Say:* What I am about to say may upset you. If so, that is not my intent. I am saying it because I believe that we cannot effectively deal with the issue unless we consider (the upsetting information).

The administrators found this heuristic useful because they often perceived others as more easily hurt than they in fact were. It helped them act, and they found that others valued the information they provided. They also learned that people usually have some idea that they have performed poorly. Failure to openly discuss performance can lead to the inference that one has performed even worse than one supposed. Participants found it helpful to consider that when they responded to their anxiety about others' possible reactions and did not provide important information, they were preventing others from improving, decreasing their own effectiveness, and creating undiscussable issues in their organization. Recognition of these consequences helped them overcome their Model I protective strategies.

The thing that seemed to worry seminar participants most as they tried to learn Model II strategies was the possibility that their Model II actions might make someone very angry or, worse yet, hurt someone. Strong reactions indicate that an issue is perceived as highly significant. It is helpful to remember that strong reactions are evoked by specific, observable events. When participants learned to interpret emotional responses as indications of how important it might be to discover what was significant about a specific event, it was easier for them to avoid reflexively acting to minimize hurt or anger. They found it useful to keep in mind that helping people deal effectively with events that produce emotional responses is helping them improve their functioning as human beings. Yet insight into how emotional reactions can ultimately help others was not sufficient for participants to overcome their reflexive action patterns. They needed a heuristic to fall back on and use initially by rote to respond to the emotional reactions of others.

Responding to Emotional Reactions

Flag: When others react to what you say with hurt or anger,

Recognize that they may have good reasons for that reaction. Also recognize that if you try to immediately minimize the hurt or anger, you are colluding to prevent that person from learning. You are also allowing others to control your actions through your fear of how they might react. This eliminates your freedom to act in ways that might be important for increasing effectiveness. If the hurt or anger seem justified,

Say: It seems to me that you were hurt (or angered) by (what I said). My intention was not to make you angry, but to deal with the issue before us. We cannot do that without talking about some things that I infer you would prefer not to hear. While it may be upsetting to do so, I believe that it is important for us to continue. What are your views?

or

If the reaction is sufficiently strong to stop further discussion, yet you don't know what is causing it, first discover its source and deal with it.

Say: (Other), help me understand. I am unable to see the reason for your hurt (anger). What is it about this situation or about what I did or said that makes you hurt (angry)?

This heuristic is designed to identify the event that caused the angry or hurt response. If the response was justified, the person who caused the emotional response should acknowledge that it was justified and then clearly state the consequences of responding solely to the emotion.

Say: I now see why you are hurt (angry). I would feel the same if I were you. However, I believe that if we respond to your hurt (anger) by stopping this discussion, we may be unable to deal effectively with the problem. Is it your wish or intent that we drop work on the problem?

This elaboration of the heuristic was designed to help participants realize that they allow others to control them when they automatically respond to emotional reactions. It showed them how to respond to others' emotionality in ways that focused on increasing effectiveness and still dealt with others' reactions. The aim of the heuristic is to avoid Model I dynamics that might obscure important information and reduce effectiveness. The point is not to ignore or try to minimize emotional reactions, but to use them as opportunities to learn about and constructively deal with the events that elicited them.

While emotional reactions usually inhibit learning, people can become skilled at using them to facilitate it. This skill is particularly valuable for dealing with the frustration, bewilderment, and anger that arise when one tries to learn about and change theories-in-use. These emotional reactions are certainly understandable. When people who are normally competent in their professional and personal lives discover not only that their actions are ineffective but that their efforts to act differently also fail, it is important for them to realize that frustration is a natural part of trying to unlearn one complex set of actions and to learn a new one. It is also important to learn how to use emotional responses to identify the specific actions that caused them. The emotion generated indicates that the action may relate to a critical aspect of a theory-in-use. Pursuing the lead provided by the emotion can bring about insight and rapid learning.

As participants in the seminar learned and practiced the segments of Model II action contained in the heuristics, their competence increased and they were able to string together longer and longer segments of effective action. As they gained ability to deal with more complex situations, they raised issues that were unique to them or to their institutions and for which no appropriate heuristics existed. When this occurred it was time for them to begin designing their own heuristics and using them to transfer their Model II skills outside the seminar setting.

Stage Four: Generalization. Transferring Skills to the Institutional Setting

The transfer of Model II skills to the working environment should be a natural extension of earlier stages of the learning process. The seminar participants began by bringing sample cases of their ordinary behavior to the meetings and unearthing previously obscured meanings and unintended consequences of those behaviors. They learned to use heuristics to plan and enact behaviors with different inherent meanings in order to produce more desirable effects. In so doing, they discovered the flaws in their current action patterns, planned changes, and used heuristics provided by the instructor to enact those changes. All this occurred at a pace that maximized effectiveness by minimizing pressure and anxiety.

When seminar members became able to independently analyze a situation and then design and enact behavior to produce more desirable consequences, they could use Model II to solve their own problems. Fostering independent problem solving is the primary aim of this stage of learning. Each participant brought recurrent, complex problems in the work environment to the seminar for analysis. These problems replaced the brief written cases and short segments of interaction as the focus of seminar activity. The group employed Model I and its diagnostic methodology to understand the nature of a problem. Then the person bringing in the problem used Model II skills to design a personal heuristic for use the next time the problem arose. The personal heuristic is the device that completes the transfer of Model II skills to the work environment and makes it a natural extension of the learning exercises worked on throughout the seminar.

For a hypothetical example of how a participant might do the analysis and design, we can return to the earlier case of the president and the dean. If the president had brought the problem of the dean to the seminar during the generalization stage, he would have begun by stating his perception of the original problem: the dean could not effectively run his school and repeatedly asked the president what to do. The president would have been able to analyze the case and see that if he gave the dean the requested help, he would make the dean dependent on him. Since each request for help produced this consequence, the request for help clearly was the directly observable event most closely related to the dean's problem. That event, therefore, is the appropiate "flag" for the president's personal heuristic for reacting to the dean. Given the flag, the president would have incorporated his analysis in a "recognize" statement and used Model II behavioral strategics to design an intervention that would effectively make the dean aware of the problem.

A Personal Heuristic

Flag: When the dean asks for help,
Recognize that doing as he asks makes him dependent on you and forces you to assume his responsibilities and take initiatives for him.
Act: State and illustrate the consequences of complying with his request. Make explicit that those consequences are the real problem as you see it.
Say: Dean, the question you ask illustrates one of the problems I have. You ask me to take initiatives and responsibility for you.

The president could use this heuristic to start solving his problem with the dean the next time the flagged behavior occurs. Notice, however, that this heuristic only provides the first few statements for the president's response to the dean. The president must then respond by tacitly and automatically analyzing the situation and designing and enacting Model II behaviors in real-time. All the practice in the seminar was aimed at making these processes second nature, so that participants could function automatically, even in a high-pressure interaction.

Using a new theory-in-use in the work environment requires a great deal of practice. Some of that practice can take place in the seminar, but much more must occur in the work environment itself. Many errors are likely when a person first tries to use Model II under real conditions; however, the double-loop learning skills practiced in the seminar should help uncover mistakes and correct ineffective behavior.

Individuals must focus on two sources of ineffectiveness in their institutions. First, they must use their Model II skills of analysis and heuristic design to discover and alter single-loop problem solving and other sources of error. Second, they must do their part to change those aspects of the institution's interpersonal environment that perpetuate and reinforce single-loop and Model I actions. To do the latter requires that they use the heuristics and methods learned in the seminar to help make other members of the institution aware of the unintended consequences of their theories-in-use and to teach them an alternative model for action.

Conclusions

It should be apparent that transforming an institution from one that reinforces single-loop processes into one that facilitates double-loop learning implies transferring skills learned in seminar to one's organization and spreading Model II skills throughout the staff. The theory-of-action certainly implies that such transfer is the only way to make an institution capable of solving its own problems. The methods for effecting transfer are explicitly incorporated into the design of the learning seminar in the form of heuristics that people can use both to change their theories-in-use and to aid others to change.

This brief sampling of the course of events in teaching Model II should make it clear that these skills are not easy to acquire or to apply. It is necessary for participants to remain genuinely open to change and conscious of the difficulties involved in learning an alternative theory-of-action. They must continually test the usefulness of the approach and evaluate the extent to which it addresses their own problems. If the approach and the instructor adequately demonstrate the usefulness of the theory-of-action in these confrontations, then the learning process becomes self-reinforcing, with participants gaining greater insight into their problems and connecting those insights with patterns of action that increase their effectiveness. The approach then offers them a way to detect the roots of their problems and to use their own and other's capacities to solve problems. From a theory-of-action perspective, this is the only way to genuinely increase the effectiveness of faculty and administrators. This chapter should make it clear that such learning is difficult and painful. Only individuals deeply committed to increasing their effectiveness and convinced that Model II will do so are willing to expend the effort necessary to change their theories-in-use.

6

❖❖❖❖❖❖❖❖❖

Uses and Limitations of the Theory-of-Action Approach

❖❖❖❖❖❖❖❖❖❖❖❖❖❖❖❖❖❖❖❖❖

The reality of the change process seldom approximates the comfortable predictability of the examples given in preceding chapters. A linear path to effective change is only apparent in theory, or in a lucky case, in retrospect; the real path is characterized by diversions, false starts, and dead ends. A fair view of the theory-of-action requires us to treat some of the difficulties and uncertainties omitted earlier and respond to questions frequently raised about the approach. For example, a demonstration of how individuals at Liberal College used Model II skills to address the problems identified in Chapter Four would elegantly close this book. In reality Model II skills were never applied to those problems, so such a neat ending is not possible. Likewise, there were too many possible actions open to individuals in Liberal College to even meaningfully speculate about how they might have acted differently.

At best the analysis in Chapter Four identified some processes underlying problems in the institution. For example, the unwillingness or inability of language faculty to change their approach to their discipline went unaddressed, and the program advocates' decision to continue the funding effort without the support of the language departments inevitably created conflict, guaranteeing that faculty whose support was essential would resist the enactment of the program. A permanent solution to this problem would have required that faculty and program advocates address the characteristics of their theories-in-use that created and maintained the problem. The feasibility of that solution would have depended on participants' ability to examine their own actions, the skills of whatever development staff might have been brought in, and how strongly the problem was reinforced by the institutional system.

Previous chapters also failed to stress that institutions and individuals cannot impose a change in individuals' theories-in-use. People in the seminar described in Chapter Four freely chose to try to learn Model II and were highly committed to testing its ability to increase their effectiveness. Free choice and internal commitment create the preconditions for individuals to learn actively and to practice new behavioral strategies and governing values. Learning devices such as heuristics, however, are only temporary aids for learning to break old patterns and to practice new ones. Memorizing and using a few heuristics does not produce Model II action. Learning Model II so that it is usable in "real time" requires that one internalize the values and strategies underlying the heuristics. The sustained effort and self-examination required for tacit-level learning is only possible for persons internally committed to the effort to change. Learning seminars maximize choice and encourage continued testing of the usefulness of the theory-of-action and its ultimate effect on an organization.

Because learning new skills is difficult and extended over time, some individuals drop out before the end of a seminar or change program. Others stop after they learn the details of the approach because they are unwilling to give up unilateral control. Such individuals typically feel uncomfortable when they try to enact Model II strategies and believe such strategies will never work in the real world. Some individuals value the approach, but stop because others in their organization reject it as too risky, broad-reaching, or alien. Another reason that individuals stop learning is that they cannot detach themselves enough from the immediacy of an interaction to think about their actions. Finally, the general format of Model II seminars sometimes leads individuals to lose interest. It usually takes two or three days' intensive work interspersed with three or four months of practice on one's own to consolidate learning and uncover important issues to treat in subsequent seminars. Those not highly committed to learning avoid practicing and thinking about what they have learned. As a result they see little cumulative effect and lose interest in going further. Also the learning format produces a period of considerable frustration before the ability to analyze and design new behaviors increases. Some individuals are sufficiently satisfied with the initial increases in their effectiveness that they feel no need for further learning.

Is learning Model II worth all the effort?

From one point of view, this question relates to satisfaction with the Model II skills learned. While the number of those who have learned Model II well enough to transfer it to their organizations is small at this time, it appears that satisfaction with Model II increases as skill at using it to attack real-time problems increases. Thus, bridging the action gap is rewarding even though the effort opens a new series of challenges on how to teach Model II to subordinates and how to demonstrate that Model II is not just a gimmick or another administrative control device.

From another viewpoint satisfaction with Model II skills might be regarded as analogous to the satisfaction a surgeon feels after learning the skills needed to perform a particular operation. In this light, satisfaction would come from acquiring the skills needed to solve a specific problem. This type of satisfaction should not be expected, because Model II skills are not specific to particular kinds of problems. Rather they provide the means first to *find* existing problems, then to *design* appropriate solutions. They are general skills that should have more power because they apply to a wider variety of situations. Unlike Prisoner's Dilemma and other simulations, Model II does not prescribe specific actions. Model II solutions require in-depth learning about one's organization and its theory-in-use before trying to solve a particular problem. Those who want a toolbox of specific things to do are likely to be dissatisfied with Model II.

Finally, there is the potential dissatisfaction of being "Model II'ed" to death. One must learn when to apply Model II and when not. It is often hard to decide when the skills are most useful because some problems that are superficially simple may reflect serious errors in the institutional theory-in-use, and one would not want to miss them. On the other hand, one would not want to use Model II skills to make routine decisions such as how many paper clips to order. Satisfaction increases as one's ability to quickly detect Model II issues increases.

How does this theory-of-action approach fit into my institutional priorities?

Some recent data (Duea, 1981) on how college and university presidents rank the issues facing higher education help answer this question. Unsurprisingly, financial problems and concern over enrollment are the number one and two issues. More germane to this book was their rating of the need for program development and improvement; changing the purpose of an institution; and maintaining and reorganizing programs in response to inflation and enrollment pressures. All were among the six most pressing needs. The case of Liberal College certainly indicates the relevance of the theory-of-action to these high priority issues. The effort to create a Cultures of Europe Program was made in response to changing enrollment patterns and the need to begin new programs. The failure to understand the source of resistance to such change resulted in a large expenditure on a program that had little effect on enrollment patterns, academic programs, or faculty interests.

The notion that long-standing patterns of faculty behavior and institutional actions must change to meet current challenges seems basic to all the presidents' priorities. These changes would imply that faculty and administrators must consider solutions they might previously have rejected because they required that individuals construct new roles for themselves, their departments, and their institutions. Such solutions require the alteration of underlying assumptions and values and the abandonment of single-loop action patterns. Model II is designed specifically to address such problems, and Model II skills would appear critical to redesigning programs and making institutional changes that individuals will be internally committed to and work for rather than oppose.

Another interesting piece of data comes from the study of presidents cited above. Faculty development programs were rated thirteenth in a list of twenty most pressing institutional priorities. College presidents clearly see currently available programs for "developing" institutions of higher education as irrelevant to existing problems. Chapter One suggested several reasons why current development models have failed to help institutions solve problems, and the rest of this book suggests how the theory-of-action has the potential to overcome the inadequacies of existing approaches.

In light of the financial pressures in higher education, how is it possible to justify spending money on Model II training when the payoffs are not easily specified?

There are two kinds of organizational problems—those that irritate people and those that cost the organization money. When finances are tight, one can only address the costly ones. One of the difficulties in higher education is the inability to clearly define the cost of many problems. For example, what do unproductive faculty cost an institution? In part, it costs whatever the institution pays them in salaries, but the reduced enrollment in particular departments and the erosion of an institution's ability to attract students is another, if indeterminate cost. Departmental and administrative fights consume time better spent in revenue-producing activities and constitute another tax on an institution's scarce resources. Finally, the inability to effectively adjust to a changing environment yearly escalates costs in ways that are hard to assess, yet no less fatal if not checked.

How likely is it, then, that the theory-of-action will solve the problems in an institution?

Individuals immersed in a problem can best judge the effectiveness of an effort to solve it. The earlier presentation of the diagnostic power of the theory at Liberal College and of the Model II seminar may provide some notion of the possible usefulness and applicability of the theory. If readers recognize familiar problems in Liberal College and find that the theory-of-action analysis of them makes sense, then it may have relevance to their institution. This does not mean that the approach will automatically solve those problems, however, because too much depends on the specific problems and the skills and motivation of an institution's members.

How do I know whether my institution needs Model II and the radical change it implies?

When members of an institution feel their solutions for difficult problems are temporary, at best, and that the same old problems recur and worsen, the source of the problem is some enduring feature of the institution and its personnel. Model II is most appropriate for addressing these institutional and personal invariants. For example, Liberal College tried to reorient departments and change faculty with curricular and programmatic innovations. Departments and faculty consistently resisted. Ultimately programmatic changes were forced, but the intended benefits never emerged. Shortly after funding for Cultures of Europe lapsed, a committee analogous to the Drafting Committee proposed major changes in graduation requirements for students as a way of reorienting departmental programs and faculty. This effort to change the general college program met greater resistance than had Cultures of Europe. The resulting meetings and arguments were too familiar for many faculty. Advocates and opponents of the change responded to each other in characteristic single-loop fashion, repeatedly using the same strategy. Many individuals sensed the helpless repetition of some apparently inevitable cycle. Such awareness was one important sign that the institution was not addressing important double-loop issues.

Widespread awareness of the existence of undiscussable issues can also indicate that serious problems are being ignored. Individuals in an institution frequently know that they do not openly discuss critical issues, but they cannot clearly say what prevents the discussions. For example, one department at a large university consistently turned down proposals from one of its faculty members to add and teach new courses. The review committee told her that it rejected the proposed courses because the content was covered elsewhere in the curriculum or that a particular course's content was not appropriate for the department. In reality the committee simply felt that the faculty member was not competent to teach the courses and would not have allowed her to teach them under any circumstances. The committee's feedback to the instructor, however, focused on the course characteristics rather than her competence. As a result she continued to revise her proposals to answer the committee's objections and it repeatedly turned them down for increasingly specious reasons. The more she tried to get a course passed, the less likely it became that the committee would ever mention her competence as the reason for its decisions. Her competence was undiscussable. Members of the department were acutely aware that the situation should be changed, but they were unable to do it.

Awareness of the need to change indicates that an institution might benefit from Model II skills. Before deciding to try to learn those skills, however, it is important to learn whether members of the institution are willing to change. Unfortunately, such an assessment is often uncertain and difficult. For example, when generally competent individuals learn that their best efforts to act effectively produce consequences that are detrimental to their institution (from the theory-of-action perspective), they often react with disbelief, frustration, or anger. These understandable reactions do not necessarily indicate that they are unable or unwilling to change. In fact, a willingness to challenge the approach and demand that its validity be demonstrated is essential for effective learning of Model II. It would seem foolish to adopt a new theory-of-action without making certain that it was better than an existing one.

The distinguishing characteristic of persons able to change is that while they argue about the validity of an alternative they remain willing to change *if* they see that the new approach is better (that is, more effective) than their current one. Even though they are captives of their existing theory-in-use, people capable of change are willing to experiment, to see whether something better is possible. They may remain skeptical, but they are willing to entertain the possibility that their perceptions and interpretations incorporate a source of error that reduces the effectiveness of their actions.

Individuals unlikely to change either openly reject any possibility that they could learn to act more effectively or they do the complete opposite; that is, they publicly accept any proposed change without questioning it. The first type of individual seldom admits to making an error and is unwilling to accept advice and suggestions from others. Like all people he distorts information to fit his own interpretations. Unlike some he rejects the possibility that he is doing so. The second type of person will gladly go along with any program as long as her superiors want it. If the dean or department chairperson wants a program, this person never objects or expresses misgivings. She has no commitment to change, however, only to saluting her superior. In assessing individuals' ability to change, do not be put off by skepticism and questioning. They are essential ingredients. At the same time be wary if everyone is thrilled by the idea.

Who in my institution should learn Model II?

The objective of a Model II seminar is to teach the skills that will enable individuals to discover the roots of their problems, to design and implement solutions, and to transfer their new skills back to the institution and to other individuals who need them. Individuals in the best position to use the skills and to facilitate their transfer are the people who should first attempt to learn Model II. Chairpersons, faculty leaders, and top administrative officials best fit this description. While it may take some effort to identify the appropriate faculty leaders, the appropriate administrators are university or college presidents and academic deans because they are best informed about and most involved with creating and maintaining institution-wide change. They also lend credibility to any change effort and help to overcome initial skepticism.

From the theory-of-action perspective, this top-down approach is the most effective way to address sources of error in an institution's theory-in-use for two reasons. If the highest levels of an organization were not involved, other members of the institution would not regard the effort to solve problems deeply embedded in an organization as serious. Without the involvement of top-level administrators and faculty, people at lower levels would be likely to see any program as an effort to manipulate them rather than to increase effectiveness. Furthermore, the involvement of only lower-level members of an organization could create a disaster. If faculty and/or lower-level administrators advocated major changes in policy/ organization without the president's, deans', and chairpersons' participation, these administrative authorities might well view the proposed change as an usurpation of their prerogatives and reject it out of hand.

How can I select the program for producing change that will best address the problems my institution has?

Once an institution has decided it needs help to solve its problems, it must still select a specific program. While I have argued for a theory-of-action approach, this analysis presented suggests several important features of any program that an institution might want to evaluate. If the institution wants its members to solve their own problems, then anyone offering a change program should specify exactly what skills individuals learn during the program and how they transfer those skills from the program to their institution. In short, they should have a systematic approach for bridging the action gap. Programs not specifically designed to transfer learning back to an institution are unlikely to successfully address double-loop issues. One of the underlying causes of the contagious lack of interest in existing faculty development programs is that they cannot bridge the action gap and therefore cannot solve institutions' most serious problems.

It is also important to determine how people offering a program view the duration of their involvement, because it is an important indicator of their approach to the issue of dependence. If they suggest that their involvement might continue and become a regular part of the institution, then they see the institutions' problems as unsolvable by its members and the skills for addressing any new problems as unlearnable. They are likely to foster continued dependence on their skills.

Some programs do not investigate existing conditions in an institution and specify their view of existing problems and their causes before trying to solve the problems. Programs that do not begin with a diagnostic phase either assume that their skills will solve any problem or that the program is a universal solution. They commit an institution to potentially expensive programmatic efforts without first making sure that the capabilities of the program fit the problem. The lack of an initial diagnostic period limits the amount of information on which the institution can base its decision and increases its dependence on experts to assure them that the program will work. This approach may lead faculty and administrators to want no part of the program after only a short exposure, which means that the institution has invested its funds in an inappropriate program. Although a diagnostic period may seem like a slow approach, it maximizes the information an institution has and constitutes a clear two-step approach to any program. If an institution does not agree with the problems isolated and the solutions proposed during the diagnostic period, it can make an informed decision not to continue into another phase of change.

* * *

The notion that a college or university must exert a great deal of effort to successfully solve its problems has been implicit and explicit throughout this book. Difficult problems are deeply rooted in the complexity of institutional life. It is impossible to address one problem without either encountering or creating others. The theory-of-action approach suggests that superficially different problems all reflect an underlying institutional theory-in-use that reinforces the error-producing actions of individuals within the institution. The interrelatedness of problems at various levels of an institution makes any quick, easy, or fast-acting solutions impossible. Development teams who suggest that a change effort might produce painless change should be looked at skeptically. A basic notion in the theory-of-action approach is that lasting solutions require changes in the behavioral strategies and governing values that people and institutions use to guide their actions. It takes hard effort, practice, and commitment to accomplish that level of change. The only thing that justifies the effort is the prospect that the skills so learned will allow individuals to become their own problem solvers and to create institutional norms that foster commitment to increasing effectiveness.

Let me end with a note of caution and optimism. One possibility pointed out by some is that Model II behavior and the effectiveness it engenders are an unobtainable, overoptimistic objective. The argument goes that the world is what it is and that people either cannot or will not abandon Model I strategies and values. In such a world effectiveness means being able to achieve one's goals within the existing living system as opposed to trying to alter that system. While this means that a certain amount of ineffectiveness is inevitable, it also means that Model I actions are the only effective ones.

While it is certainly true that it is hard to learn an alternative theory-in-use, it is also true that people have done it. While it is difficult to assess the long-term effects of that learning, those involved certainly perceive themselves as more effective. At the same time they appear more aware of the necessity for continued learning and change.

Another point, however, is more important than the admittedly inconclusive results to date: If the ineffectiveness characteristic of Model I is built into existing goal-directed action in the manner that the theory-of-action suggests, then continued existence of only a Model I world will lead inevitably to increasing error, decreasing effectiveness, and diminishing ability to adapt to a changing environment. Indeed, many businesses, educational organizations, and government bureaucracies are characterized by decreasing productivity and increasing entropy that are entirely consistent with this analysis. To the extent that the foregoing analysis is true, the only way to address the roots of these problems is to alter the theory-in-use producing them. If existing problems cannot be solved without a new model for human action, then that new model is both pragmatically and ethically essential. That this may mean major change in the existing organizational world is a distinct possibility. That it is hard to construct that changed world is irrelevant. That the technology for teaching a new model of action needs development is a challenge well worth answering. That such change might be possible is a source of optimism and a goal worth the investment of considerable energy, intellect, and effort.

References

Argyris, C. *Intervention: Theory and Practice.* Reading, Mass.: Addison-Wesley, 1970.

Argyris, C. *Increasing Leadership Effectiveness.* New York: Wiley-Interscience, 1976.

Argyris, C., and Schön, D. *Theory in Practice: Increasing Professional Effectiveness.* San Francisco: Jossey-Bass, 1974.

Argyris, C., and Schön, D. *Organizational Learning: A Theory of Action Perspective.* Reading, Mass.: Addison-Wesley, 1978.

Bergquist, W. H., and Phillips, S. R. "Components of an Effective Faculty Development Program." *The Journal of Higher Education,* 1975a, *46,* 177–211.

Bergquist, W. H., and Phillips, S. R. *A Handbook for Faculty Development.* Vol. 1. Washington, D.C.: Council for the Advancement of Small Colleges, 1975b.

Bergquist, W. H., and Phillips, S. R. *A Handbook for Faculty*

Development. Vol. 2. Washington, D.C.: Council for the Advancement of Small Colleges, 1977.

Bergquist, W. H., and Shoemaker, W. A. (Eds.). *New Directions for Higher Education: A Comprehensive Approach to Institutional Development,* no. 15. San Francisco: Jossey-Bass, 1976.

Centra, J. A. *Faculty Development Practices in U.S. Colleges and Universities.* Princeton, N.J.: Educational Testing Service, 1976.

Centra, J. A. "Pluses and Minuses for Faculty Development." *Change,* 1977, *9,* 47–48, 64.

Duea, J. "Presidents' Views on Current and Future Issues in Higher Education." *Phi Delta Kappan,* 1981, *62,* 586–588.

Gaff, J. G. *Toward Faculty Renewal: Advances in Faculty, Instructional, and Organizational Development.* San Francisco: Jossey-Bass, 1975.

Gaff, J. G. (Ed.). *New Directions for Higher Education: Institutional Renewal Through the Improvement of Teaching,* no. 24. San Francisco: Jossey-Bass, 1978.

Nisbett, R. E., and Wilson, T. D. "Telling More Than We Can Know: Verbal Reports on Mental Processes." *Psychological Review,* 1977, *84,* 231–259.

Polanyi, M. *Personal Knowledge: Towards a Post-Critical Philosophy.* Chicago: University of Chicago Press, 1958.

Polanyi, M. *The Tacit Dimension.* New York: Doubleday, 1967.

Index

123